Christmas 2010

Scott

Welcome to Los Angeles!
Thanks for the great work
you are doing at 1st church.

All my best!

Bob Smiland

CLASSIC HOMES
OF
LOS ANGELES

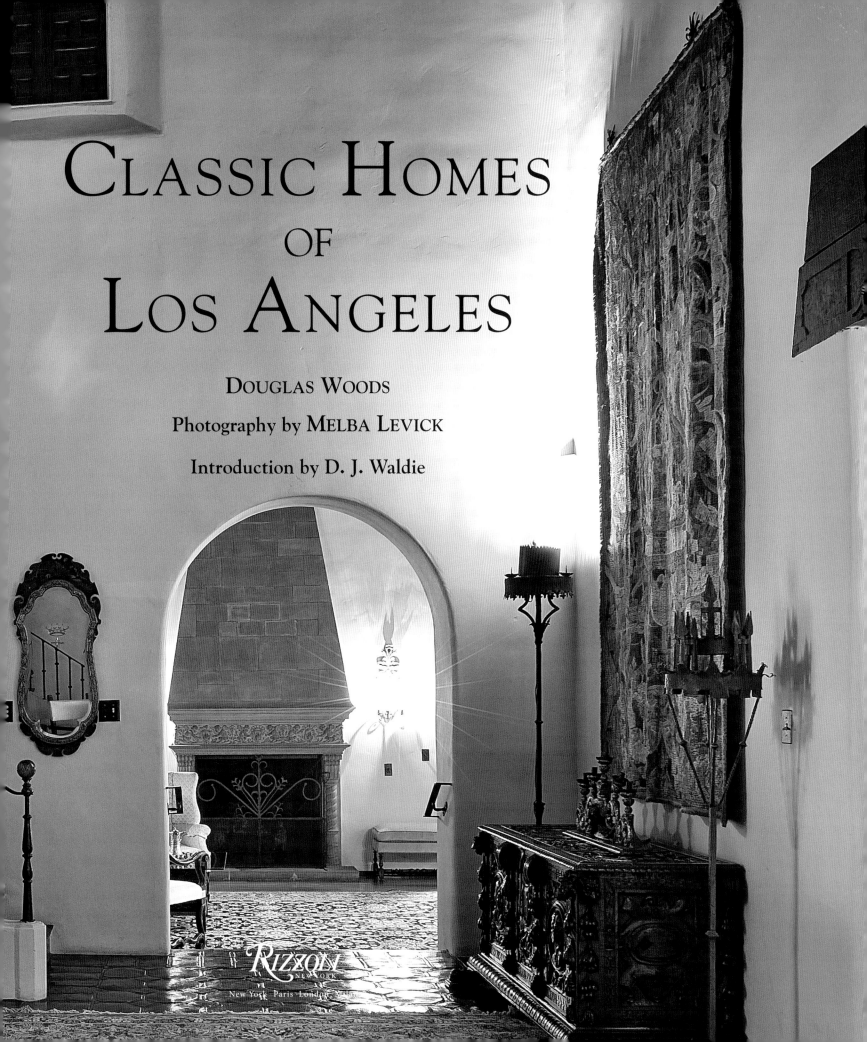

CLASSIC HOMES
OF
LOS ANGELES

DOUGLAS WOODS

Photography by MELBA LEVICK

Introduction by D. J. Waldie

RIZZOLI
NEW YORK

New York Paris London Milan

For Allegra — DW

For my mother and father — ML

First published in the United States of America in 2010 by
RIZZOLI INTERNATIONAL PUBLICATIONS, INC.
300 Park Avenue South, New York, NY 10010
www.rizzoliusa.com

ISBN-13: 978-0-8478-3384-9
Library of Congress Control Number: 2010920883

Distributed to the U.S. Trade by
Random House, New York

Design: ABIGAIL STURGES
Assistant Editor: JOHN MCINTYRE

Printed and bound in China

2010 2011 2012 2013 2014 2015/
10 9 8 7 6 5 4 3 2 1

PAGE 1 *Adamson House (Hancock Park),
doorway gate and grille (p. 124)*

PAGES 2–3 *Prindle House, living room (p. 196)*

PAGE 4 *Adamson House (Malibu), tile detail (p. 134)*

Contents

Preface

Most of the homes featured in this book are situated in the historic residential core of Los Angeles, stretching west from downtown through the West Adams district to Hancock Park and Windsor Square. With the exception of one in Beverly Hills, the rest are located in the neighboring communities of La Canada Flintridge, Pasadena, and San Marino, independent municipalities closely tied to Los Angeles and known for their high concentration of well-preserved period architecture.

Southern California has seen the growth of numerous grass roots preservation groups whose work, in recent decades, has helped to preserve our built environment and, in turn, our heritage. In particular, the Los Angeles Conservancy has done much to raise public appreciation for the comparatively short, yet rich, architectural history of the city. Homeowners, such as those individuals who participated in this book, should be commended as well for being good stewards and for demonstrating how a house can take on twenty-first-century amenities while, at the same time, maintaining its historical integrity. Los Angeles has always been a hotbed of architectural experimentation and it will continue to be such. The hope is that as the city develops and grows denser it will find ways to protect its past as well.

Writer's Studio, Cecil B. DeMille Estate

Introduction: A Dream of Home

D. J. WALDIE

Los Angeles was, above all, at the end of a continent, at the end of the line, and, even at the end of the nineteenth century, a destination both exotic and a little unreal. Los Angeles in 1890 was part mirage, overlooking its wide, nearly empty plain, and part chimera—a place of so many disparate parts, and all of them lacking the steadying traditions of New York or Boston or the self-confident and boisterous shouldering-aside arrogance of Chicago. Los Angeles on the threshold of the new century was a small, dusty place, a languid place, a place offering domestic retreat for those earnestly seeking some form of redemption—from tubercular lungs, broken spirits, or the post-traumatic stresses of America's clamorous Gilded Age. Los Angeles then was west of everything American, but not actually in the West, not where the exhilarating life of breaking the plains, extending Manifest Destiny, and opening the frontier was just ending. Los Angeles was south of that West, a tan and gray-green island remote from the urban centers of the East. It was semitropic, too—a country of golden oranges, thick hanging grapes, roses in midwinter, and geraniums blooming all year long. Like the tropics, it seemed lush and yielding, but its hills and arroyos could burn with electric suddenness, roil violently in an earthquake, slip into sheets of adobe mud with every sudden rain, or wallow in floods that every decade turned the region into a vast shallow lake.

More than the landscape was potentially treacherous. Los Angeles was a place whose history as a Spanish and Mexican colonial outpost seemed all too present at the beginning of the twentieth century, almost ready to overwhelm the starched Midwest conventions that its American possessors brought here. Yet the Hispanic past of Los Angeles was nearly ungraspable and mostly unusable as material for a narrative that must include both Mexicans and Michiganders, mestizo laborers and Anglo entrepreneurs, the remnants of a fading culture of Catholicism and hospitality and a brash new American culture given to competition and display. The novelist Helen Hunt Jackson had tried in *Ramona* (first serialized in 1884) to reconcile the conflicted meanings of Los Angeles, a place that was immemorial in the rhythms of its life and as aggressively up-to-date as any chamber of commerce member would want.

Jackson saw beauty and moral order in the primal materials of Spanish and Mexican Los Angeles, and wrote a romantic fable into which she breathed the undying life of myth. She gave value to the ease and comfort that was latent in the Los Angeles landscape, and began the unfinished task of making Southern California fully part of the American experience. But Jackson did not make Los Angeles her home. She died soon after *Ramona* became a national sensation. And she would not have welcomed the ways in which her story came to romanticize real estate more than the lives of the indigenous peoples of Southern California.

Mythic *Ramona* drew those who followed Jackson here, a well-read copy of her novel and a flyer from a Los Angeles land company in hand. The forms their dreams took have given Los Angeles and its suburbs a remarkable architectural legacy, but one still entangled with unanswered longing for a sense of place.

The aesthetics of desire

By 1910, Los Angeles had boomed and busted and begun again to accumulate wealth in the form of oil and agriculture and preeminently as real estate. A wealthy stratum of Los Angeles society could aspire to grand houses, but they were a decidedly mixed band of dreamers.

Edward L. Doheny was self-made, rising from prospector and frontier surveyor to oil tycoon by drilling the city's first successful well in 1893 and launching a boom in petroleum that continued through the 1920s. Doheny was a rough man, Wisconsin born and shaped by successive business failures until a chance discovery made him rich. David B. Gamble and his family were rich already through their dutiful stewardship of the Proctor & Gamble Company. Like many of the East Coast rich, they made a winter home in sunny Pasadena, their dreams tempered by the ideals of the Arts & Crafts movement. Henry William O'Melveny was a native Angeleño who moved among the city's new Anglo elite as lawyer, investor, and civic leader. His wealth came through his shrewd judgments about the golden future of Southern California. He needed a house as sober he. William Andrews Clark, Jr., only son of robber baron William Andrews Clark, founded the Los

Earl Estate, courtyard patio

Doheny Mansion, view of tower

A Dream of California

Except for the underappreciated Irving Gill, whose lucid modernity was mostly local and self-taught, the architects who embodied the city's dream of home returned again and again to traditional European models, but more critically in the years around World War I. Los Angeles imagined itself to be the apex of Anglo-Saxon civilization, but how it chose to shelter itself began to look to other cultures—to Italy, Spain, and even Mexico, and Morocco—for ways to make a home in the sun. West of the city's urban core, in the suburbs made possible by the automobile and Henry Huntington's streetcars, modest Palladian villas, suitable for the Tuscan countryside, were succeeded by rambling estates suitable for the Hollywood hills. Imitation wasn't the aim, and authenticity had never been. What was genuine in these houses was a special Southern Californian feeling for light and air and the unassuming presence of the out-of-doors. Confidently, clients and architects worked out a vocabulary of human-scaled shapes, hand-wrought details, and rhythmic arrangements of indoor and outdoor space that hinted of Andalusia, North Africa, and even Mexican California. In the Spanish Colonial Revival style, with its appeal to an imagined past, a different kind of Modernism took shape in Los Angeles, less analytical than its rigorous European counterpart, more domestic, and above all, thoroughly romantic. Romance has been the persistent dream of Los Angeles, and now, cool, spacious, and inviting houses in the Spanish style put romance at the service of a new way of living.

Octavius Morgan, a principal in the Los Angeles architectural firm of Morgan, Walls & Clement, built such a house in 1928—as modest in scale as the colonial haciendas from which the layout of the house had come. Not at all grand, but deeply satisfying as a space for domestic life, the Morgan House exemplifies the refinement of a style that comes from subtraction. The Morgan House is beautiful because it is simple. Far more imposing and formal is the house in an eclectic Spanish-Moresque style that George Washington Smith built for the Prindles in 1926. Like many of Smith's clients, the Prindles had toured Spain and North Africa, taking photographs of architectural features, acquiring antique building elements, and buying interior decorations. In effect, the Prindles curated their house, collaborating with Smith in a design that matured over several years. But they were not unique in their level of connoisseurship. Architects as diverse in their practice and aspirations as Paul Williams, Frank Lloyd Wright, and Roland Coate found wealthy Angeleños with the taste and knowledge to commission a classic Los Angeles home.

A new conception of pleasure

The Los Angeles of cliché is a gaudy simulacrum of a real place, as shallow and flimsy as a Hollywood set, with reliable sunshine the only redeeming quality. And in its choice of domestic arrangements, the city was often called monstrous. "Only dynamite would be of any use against the Mexican ranch houses, Samoan huts, Mediterranean

Angeles Philharmonic, collected rare books, and dreamed of eighteenth-century England. When he housed his collections, it was in a fantasy. And Henry Huntington—richest of all of these by far—was shrewd, married well, and able to propel the future of Los Angeles by force of his will. His house—rather his mansion—wedded a formal English country house with interiors of French Rococo exuberance to assert dynastic continuity in a place where everyone was new made.

All the best Los Angeles houses of that era reveal the anxiousness behind their facades. Grand, knowing, well-formed—and in the case of the Gamble House, nearly perfect—the first classic homes of Los Angeles strove to marry native desire and aesthetics drawn mostly from alien forms.

villas, Egyptian and Japanese temples, Swiss chalets, Tudor cottages, and every possible combination of these styles," scolded an incendiary Nathanael West in *Day of the Locust*. West was merely echoing dismissals of Los Angeles that were already half a century old. But the lurid spectacle of Hollywood, as is often claimed, did not end the tradition of indigenous architecture that extends from the house of *arroyo* boulders hand built by Charles Fletcher Lummis in 1898 through the bungalows of the Greene brothers to the Spanish Colonial Revival houses that Wallace Neff and his many contemporaries designed through the 1920s. The jostling presence of these homes across mile after mile of Los Angeles suburb was complicated by changing taste, a desire for novelty, and even more by their owners' anxieties of social legitimacy.

Today, the harmonies are clearer. Even a house as idiosyncratic as Frank Lloyd Wright's Millard House/La Miniatura from 1923 reconnects to the experience of Los Angeles through a recurring theme of the city's domestic architecture—it is a house made for almost hermetic privacy, a house solely for inward dreaming. The houses that followed in the 1930s—houses like those Roland Coate designed for the Fudger and Garrett families—modulate with greater restraint the play of public and private space. These houses updated the homegrown Modernism that had been latent in earlier classic Los Angeles homes. In the years just after World War II, the idea of these Los Angeles houses would become the model for a suburbanizing nation. Something of the character of Los Angeles went east with the Los Angeles house—acceptance of ad hoc uses of space, social informality, and a new conception of pleasure—pleasure in the form of play and an easy accommodation to desires of everyday life. There is something of Los Angeles in nearly every postwar American home.

Making a Classic

What makes a classic home of Los Angeles? Those that sympathetically embrace the fundamentals of life here: light, air, landscape … and romance. To house these qualities—half real and half imagined—architects and their clients in the first half of the twentieth century turned to various pasts that were not their own, but without turning away from the future they thought Los Angeles represented. For the most part, they declined to engage in the culture wars of Modernism (although many great Modernist homes are part of the city's architectural heritage). Some Angeleños thought houses had other, more consoling work to do. A house that can dream for and with its owners, that can dream of both escape and shelter, makes it a classic of Los Angeles.

And, of course, a classic home must persist through time. It must still shelter succeeding owners, however footloose each successor will have been … and will be. In a classic home, easily disappointed Angeleños find enough reasons to be satisfied, if only temporarily.

Kevin Starr, the preeminent historian of California's dreams, has argued that Los Angeles is not just a place on the edge of the continent, but a whole civilization, an entire way of life, though still not fully realized. And homes are its necessary expression. How we make our home here is how we make ourselves and make some attempt at forming a moral imagination that can be fitted to the circumstances of Los Angeles. Every attempt is partial, of course, and mixed in its intentions, as even the most perfect design reveals. But every attempt at home answers someone's need, evokes someone's desire, and reciprocates someone's love. The classic home achieves another goal. Like all the homes in this survey of Los Angeles, a classic continues unceasingly to show us how to make a home here.

BELOW *Morgan House, window detail*

FOLLOWING PAGES *Earl Estate, sitting area detail*

Doheny Mansion, 1899

CHESTER PLACE
THEODORE EISEN AND SUMNER HUNT, ARCHITECTS

ABOVE *Detail, Pompeian Room*

RIGHT *The great hall, transformed by
Wallace Neff and H. Arthur Mann into
a Georgian salon*

Edward L. Doheny's story, from penniless prospector to oil titan,
is truly legendary. After failing to find success at mining silver
in New Mexico, Doheny moved his family to Los Angeles in
1891, drawn in part by the real estate boom. Unhappily, he discovered
upon his arrival that the boom had collapsed and in those tough times,
he had to figure out a way to make a living. Doheny's experience with
soil, first working for the U.S. Geological Survey and later as a miner,
suddenly paid off when he discovered pitch in the soil west of downtown Los Angeles near Echo Park. Through a $400 loan secured by
old friend Charles Canfield, he leased the spot and hastily dug the first
commercial oil well in Los Angeles, in turn setting off the Southern
California oil boom. Nearly 40 years of age and barely into his second
year in Southern California, Doheny was on his way to becoming one
of the wealthiest men in America.

In 1901, Doheny, with his new wife, Estelle, bought the house at 8
Chester Place, in the West Adams district near what is now the campus of the University of Southern California. The mansion was built
for mining executive Oliver P. Posey, but from then forward it was
known as the Doheny Mansion.

Originally designed by architects Theodore Eisen and Sumner
Hunt, the house combines a variety of Renaissance Revival and Gilded
Age Gothic styles. The steep pitched roof of clay tiles and the stuccoed

walls offer a nod to old California and the missions. The interiors of the home were especially unpleasing to Mrs. Doheny, and she spent decades exploring ways to bring more light inside while making room for her ever growing collection of rare books. The most notable interior addition is the "Pompeian Room," designed by Alfred S. Rosenheim in 1913. Its pitched dome of glass, marble columns, and Roman reproductions replaced an outdoor patio. Other additions to the property included a palm house and an adjoining pavilion with a bowling alley. In 1933, architect Wallace Neff was commissioned to oversee repairs to the mansion after the Long Beach Earthquake. Working with Neff and decorator H. Arthur Mann, Mrs. Doheny took the opportunity to transform the interiors into the more Neoclassical theme that remains today.

By the time of her passing, Estelle Doheny had weathered the tragic murder of her son, endured with her still grieving husband the Teapot Dome scandal, and, in a cruel irony for a bibliophile, fought her own bout with glaucoma, which left her almost completely blind. Her generosity to the church was unwavering throughout her life. She gave her books, including one of 48 known surviving copies of the Gutenberg Bible, to St. John's Seminary in Camarrillo, California, and had a Wallace Neff–designed library built on the grounds to house the collection. Sadly, St. John's saw fit to auction off the collection in 1985. Left by Mrs. Doheny to the Catholic Church, Chester Place is now the Doheny Campus of Mount St. Mary's College. Preserved by the college, the Doheny Mansion is open to the public for docent-led tours and chamber music concerts presented by The Da Camera Society.

FACING PAGE *Dining room*

RIGHT *Pompeian room and its glass dome, attributed to Louis Comfort Tiffany*

FOLLOWING PAGES *Stained glass ceiling detail, the Pompeian Room*

ABOVE AND RIGHT *Wallace Neff and H. Arthur Mann transformed the Doheny music room into a bright Rococo salon.*

23

Gless-Bullock House, 1916

WINDSOR SQUARE
HEINEMAN & HEINEMAN, ARCHITECTS

ABOVE *Detail, the east entrance*

RIGHT *Inglenook, with Stickley chairs*

As the story goes, this interesting Craftsman Style house was purchased by John G. Bullock in 1924 as a wedding present for his daughter, who apparently couldn't live without it—but who also couldn't live in it where it was; so, Bullock had it moved west, down Wilshire Boulevard, to its present location in Windsor Square. Though there were trucks capable of doing this at the time, the practice then was to use horse-drawn flatbeds to avoid running the risk of slipping a gear and jostling the house, possibly destroying it.

John G. Bullock founded the Bullock's department stores downtown in 1907 with then-partner Arthur Letts, a pioneering Los Angeles businessman in his own right. For nearly 90 years, the Bullock's chain dominated the full-line retail market in the west. Its iconic Art Deco flagship location, Bullocks Wilshire, a treasured landmark designed by John and Donald Parkinson in 1929, is now home to the Southwestern Law School.

The Gless-Bullock House was designed by brothers Arthur S. and Alfred Heineman. Chicago transplants, the Heineman brothers arrived in Pasadena with their parents in 1894. After trying their hands at real estate speculation, the brothers gravitated to building. Neither one, however, had been formally trained as an architect. Self taught, the talented Arthur managed to pass architecture certification exams, and in 1909 formed an official partnership with his brother, who served as his uncertified associate. Their prolific output over the following 30 years produced many homes in Pasadena and Los Angeles. Alfred's

ABOVE *Fireplace surmounted by "pulpit" balcony, which reveals Craftsman and Prairie Style detailing*

RIGHT *The dining room, with stained glass by the Judson Studios*

FOLLOWING PAGES *Detail of stained glass by the Judson Studios*

Rear view of the house, with landscaping by Sandy Kennedy

ability to design almost on the level of the Greene brothers for a lot less money than them furthered his popularity. He also sold his designs through the Sweets catalog, resulting in Heineman homes popping up around the country.

This house is an imaginative take on the classic California Craftsman style with Tudor elements and hints of the Prairie Style. The detailing in the rambling three-story teak interior is more reminiscent of something one would see in the Alps than the subtle Japanese influence we are used to seeing in the Greenes' work. Illustrating the tale of Old King Cole, the stained glass in the dining room is by the Judson Studios, the venerable stained-glass studio founded in downtown Los Angeles by English-born artist William Lees Judson and his three sons in the mid-1890s. They are still in business today. The landscaping was researched, designed, and realized by Sandy Kennedy, who specialized in the reconstruction and conservation of historical landscapes, including the A. E. Hansen garden at the mayor's mansion (Getty House), in Windsor Square.

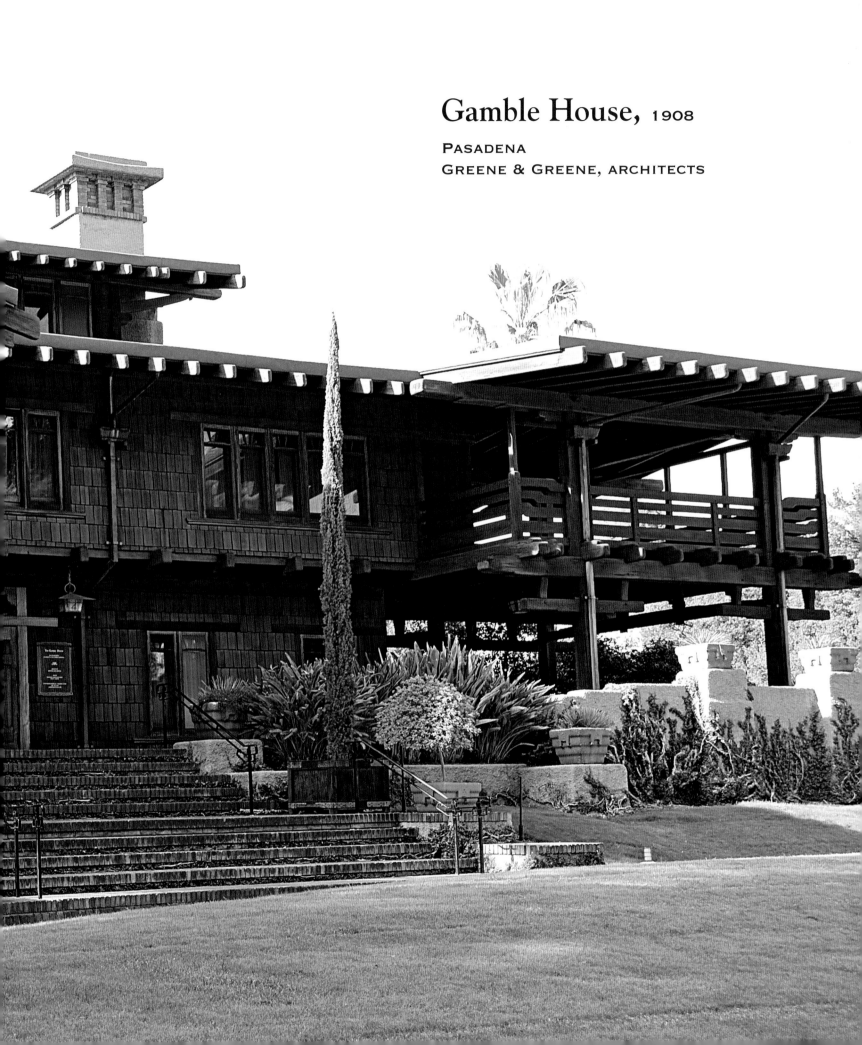

Gamble House, 1908

PASADENA
GREENE & GREENE, ARCHITECTS

ABOVE *Brick fireplace reveals fine attention to detail that is everywhere evident in this Arts & Crafts masterpiece*

RIGHT *Inglenook with tiled hearth and furniture designed by the Greene brothers*

Transplants from Cincinnati, David and Mary Gamble bought land in 1908 in Pasadena intending to build their retirement home. Brothers Charles Sumner and Henry Mather Greene had designed homes in and around Pasadena during the previous five years and were possibly on the Gambles' radar, or they met because the brothers were building a home next door for John Cole. Either way, the couple hired the brothers to build their house.

David Gamble, of the Proctor & Gamble families, had considerable resources, and the Greene brothers made great use of it. One wonders if the Gambles knew in advance that they were to end up with a masterpiece.

The Gamble House is the gold standard by which all Arts & Crafts homes are now measured. Between 1908 and 1910 the house was completed and outfitted with custom-built furniture, cabinetry, paneling, woodcarvings, lighting, and stained glass from the Greenes' studio, a quintessential example of the Arts & Crafts tradition in practice. As the Adamson beach house is a shrine to tile, the Gamble House is a temple to wood. Teak, maple, oak, cedar, and mahogany are married in beautiful interlocking joinery. The fine carpentry was done by John

LEFT *The dining room*

ABOVE *Dining room detail, showing art glass vases and exquisite leaded glass windows*

and Peter Hall, with whom the Greenes had worked before. As part of their unique take on the Craftsman style, the Greene brothers incorporated a subtle Japanese aesthetic that paid great attention to detail. That the Halls were able to so deftly execute the work is remarkable.

The porches and patio of the house's exterior are essentially outdoor rooms. That the Greenes understood how to take advantage of the climate and promote indoor-outdoor living is an understatement. The clinker brickwork on the back patio and pond seems to melt and join the house and landscape.

The house remained in the Gamble family until 1966 when Cecil and Louise Gamble deeded the house to the city of Pasadena and the University of California School of Architecture. In 1977, it was declared a national historic landmark and today is open for tours.

ABOVE *Stained glass detail, revealing a subtle palette and great artistry that is evident throughout the house*

RIGHT *Staircase and seating area demonstrating impeccable tongue and groove joinery by brothers John and Peter Hall*

FOLLOWING PAGES *Stained glass detail highlights Asian-design influences that are felt throughout the house*

TOP *Desk, designed by the Greene brothers*

ABOVE *The pantry, generous
in size for its day, was beautifully designed—
especially notable in a service room.*

RIGHT *The light and airy kitchen is a departure
from the cramped quarters common for kitchens
of the day.*

FOLLOWING PAGES *Rear view of the house,
with clinker brick wall connecting garden to house*

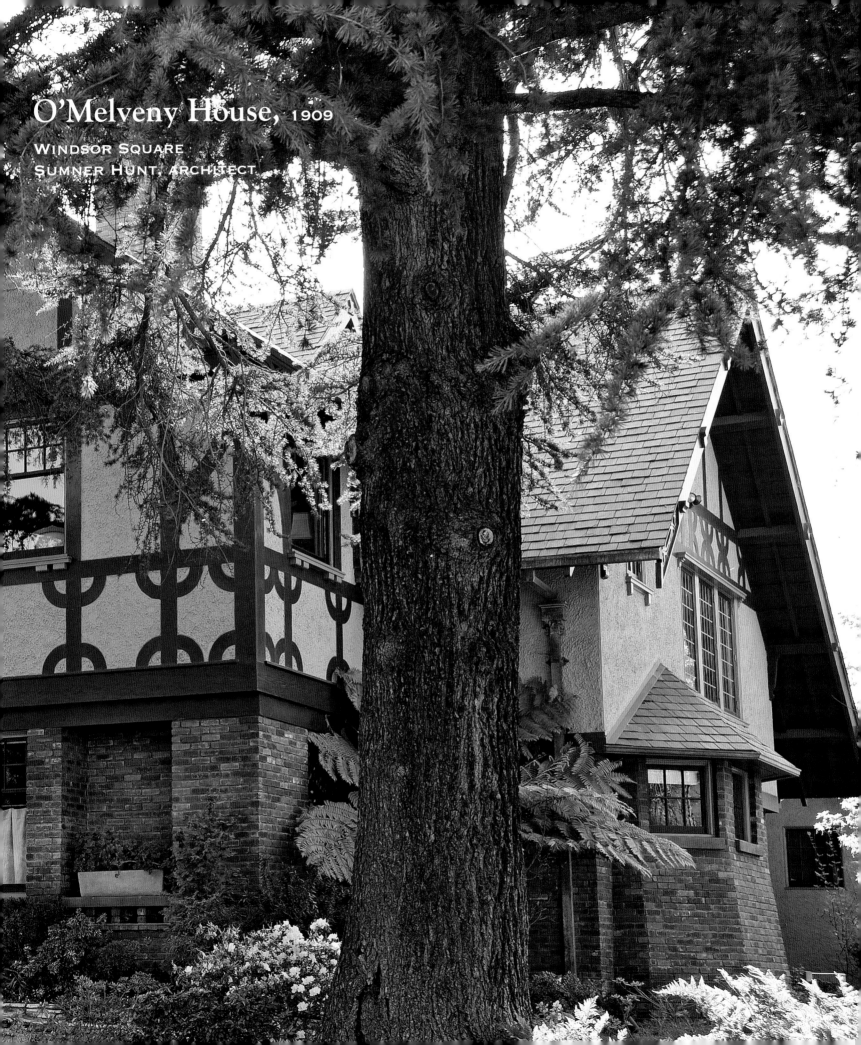

O'Melveny House, 1909
Windsor Square
Sumner Hunt, Architect

ABOVE AND RIGHT *The formal entry and foyer*

H enry O'Melveny, an Illinois native, migrated with his family to Los Angeles in 1869. He became a member of the first class of Los Angeles High School, and graduated from the University of California, Berkeley, in 1879. In 1881, he was accepted into the Los Angeles bar. He found work as an attorney at the offices of S. C. Hubbell, but was quickly recruited by Bicknell & White, an already prestigious firm specializing in real estate (partner John Dustin Bicknell went on to be a founding partner of another important firm, Gibson, Dunn & Crutcher). O'Melveny's association with these influential figures propelled him into the center of power in Southern California. It wasn't long before O'Melveny set out on his own, forming a partnership with another brilliant lawyer and real estate man, Jackson Graves.

The office of O'Melveny & Graves opened on Spring Street in downtown Los Angeles in 1885. The partners were instrumental in sorting out the mess of land ownership issues involving the dividing of the Spanish ranchos. In 1891, they shepherded the formation of the San Gabriel Water Project, which diverted a great Southern California river to create hydroelectric power, a major development for the growth of Los Angeles. It's worth noting that electricity from this project also powered Henry Huntington's fleet of red and yellow trolleys. Significantly, O'Melveny oversaw the forming of the Pacific Light & Power Company and, as well, in 1907, the forming of the Southern

PRECEDING PAGES *Formerly O'Melveny's home office, this room is now used as a library and sitting room.*

RIGHT *Dining room, with one of the five fireplaces*

FOLLOWING PAGES *In a formal departure from rest of the house, the white living room boasts eighteenth- and nineteenth-century French antiques.*

California Gas Company. He was director of the Los Angeles Public Library and a founder of the University of California, Los Angeles. O'Melveny's firm, known today as O'Melveny & Myers, eventually grew to become one of the largest and most prestigious in the world.

In 1908, O'Melveny hired the architectural firm of Hunt, Eager & Burns to build a large residence on the corner of S. New Hampshire Avenue and Wilshire Boulevard. Sumner Hunt was a popular architect amongst Los Angeles society and a great talent. His long career included designing many of the great clubhouses in Southern California and a number of mansions in the then-fashionable West Adams district near downtown. Hunt designed a three-story 15-room Medieval Revival–style house notable for its tall brick chimneys and interesting Tudor half timbering. One wing on the first floor, with its separate entrance opposite the front door, was dedicated to O'Melveny's home office.

Living on Wilshire Boulevard, already well on its way to becoming Southern California's Champs-Élysées, proved too intrusive, and in 1930, the O'Melvenys decided it was time to move west to Windsor Square, just east of Hancock Park. Toward this end, the house was divided into 3 large pieces, chimneys and all, and moved by teams of horses down Wilshire. Thus the house was moved. The transplanted structure incorporated a new full basement, garage, and staff quarters, designed by architect Gordan Kaufmann. The practice of house moving was not uncommon at this time. Families were known to have "moving parties" inside their homes as they were being tugged down the boulevard, though it is not known if the lawyer and his family partook in such festivities.

Today, the house has been restored to its intended state by preservationist Brett Waterman who oversaw everything, from regrouting the extensive brickwork and restoring all the original doors and windows to replacing the slate roof, restoring all seven of the original baths to their original condition, and rebuilding the five tall chimneys that had toppled in the 1994 Northridge earthquake. Waterman also tastefully replanted the landscape that had been taken over by a wild banana grove. Not only does the house look much like it probably did in its heyday, but it also appears as if it has always been where it sits.

Huntington Mansion, 1911

ABOVE *Alcove in hall with decorative urn flanked by fluted columns, topped by Corinthian capitals*

RIGHT *The grand entry hall*

Henry E. Huntington's roots in Southern California date back to the 1890s when he worked with his uncle Collis P. Huntington at the Southern Pacific Railway. His first great involvement with Los Angeles was the purchase and expansion of the Los Angeles Railway system know as the Yellow Cars. He later created the Pacific Electric Railway, known as the Red Car system. These two rail lines formed a sprawling public transportation system, much missed today.

By 1905, the year that Huntington and partners A. Kingsley Macomber and William R. Staats were developing the exclusive Oak Knoll subdivision just outside of Pasadena, he was busy planting the grounds of the former San Marino Ranch, which he had purchased a couple of years prior. These gardens would grow to become world famous.

The centerpiece of the property was to be a grand home for Huntington and his new wife, Arabella. Huntington drew the first sketch of the house himself and commissioned engineer Edward S. Cobb to make it buildable. (Cobb is noteworthy for having engineered Angel's Flight, the famous Los Angeles funicular railway.) Three years later he hired esteemed Los Angeles architects Myron Hunt and Elmer Grey to

ABOVE *Mantelpiece detail with gilded clock and mirror*

RIGHT *The dining room, with a Gilbert Stuart portrait of George Washington over the fireplace*

The oak paneled library and, at corner of room, one of the Boucher designed Beauvais tapestries

make the house a reality. The result is a stately Mediterranean home of mainly Italian influence. Towering toward the gardens, the south facade features a pile of steps reminiscent of Palladio.

The interiors of the house were principally designed by brothers Joseph and Charles Duveen, who became well known for importing fine and decorative art from Europe, which can now be found in many great American collections. The Duveens borrowed Classical details from French and English sources and were less sparing in their use of ornament than architects Hunt and Grey. Sir Charles Allom, of White, Allom & Company, designed the rich paneling of the period rooms envisioned by the Duveens, along with Huntington's wife, Arabella. Allom and the Duveens had gained experience creating grand interiors for such clients as Henry Clay Frick. Over the following years, Joseph Duveen continued his relationship with the Huntingtons,

FOLLOWING PAGES
*The large drawing room,
where Thomas Gainsborough's
Blue Boy once hung, when
the Huntingtons resided in
the house. The painting now
hangs in the nearby Thornton
Portrait Gallery.*

famously selling them important paintings, including Thomas Gainsborough's *Blue Boy* in 1921.

Before long it became apparent that the mansion's library would be
unable to absorb the collection of books and manuscripts Huntington
was amassing. As the gardens grew, Hunt was engaged by Huntington
again and, by 1925, he completed an imposing Beaux Arts structure to
house the extraordinary collection of rare books and French paintings.

Deeded to the public, the estate and its world-renowned gardens
continue to evolve. The house has been structurally retrofitted and
redesigned as a gallery by the Earl Corporation and the Architectural
Resources Group. The Huntington Library, with its continuing empha-
sis on British and American history and literature, fifteenth-century
European books, and the history of science, is now one of the largest
research libraries of its kind in the United States.

ABOVE *Exterior covered porch with coffered ceiling and stately colonnaded surround*

FACING PAGE *Gazebo with Classical motifs in the Rose Garden*

Jewett House, 1915

PASADENA
MARSTON & VAN PELT, ARCHITECTS

ABOVE AND RIGHT *Marston's use of yellow plays well in the golden Southern California sunlight and melds the house and garden.*

FOLLOWNG PAGES *The reflecting pond filled with water lilies*

Sylvanus B. Marston established his architectural practice in Pasadena in 1908, early in the city's social and civic development. The stamp he left on Pasadena is perhaps more indelible than that of any other architect. Throughout his career he would build civic and commercial structures, churches, and hundreds of fine homes in and around the area. Early on, Marston cultured an affinity for the Arts & Crafts movement. He designed many Craftsman Style bungalows, including his own. In 1909, he developed the St. Francis Court, the first bungalow court in the United States. He was not, however, a purist. Unlike the Greene brothers, who shunned period-revival architecture, Marston embraced it. Through the '20s and '30s, he mastered and built in all of the traditional revival styles for clients whose taste leaned more toward the Beaux Arts or Colonial. He, along with partner Garrett Van Pelt and later Edgar Maybury, built many of Southern California's finest homes.

This august Palladian-style villa is as good an example of Marston's grand revival work as one might find. Once situated on nine acres, the lot has been whittled down to around two and a half, but the house still sits behind elaborate iron gates at the end of a long tree-lined driveway surrounded by gardens and a large reflecting pool. Marston pioneered the use of exterior color in Mediterranean-style homes, and it is believed the yellow plastering here is original, or modeled after the original palet.

William Kennon Jewett, a native of Youngstown, Ohio, commissioned the house. An heir to a railroad fortune, Mr. Jewett was also president of the London Mines Company of Colorado, a huge gold mining operation. The current owners are passionate about reviving the estate to its former glory. They hope to expand the grounds and are working to restore the interior down to the last detail.

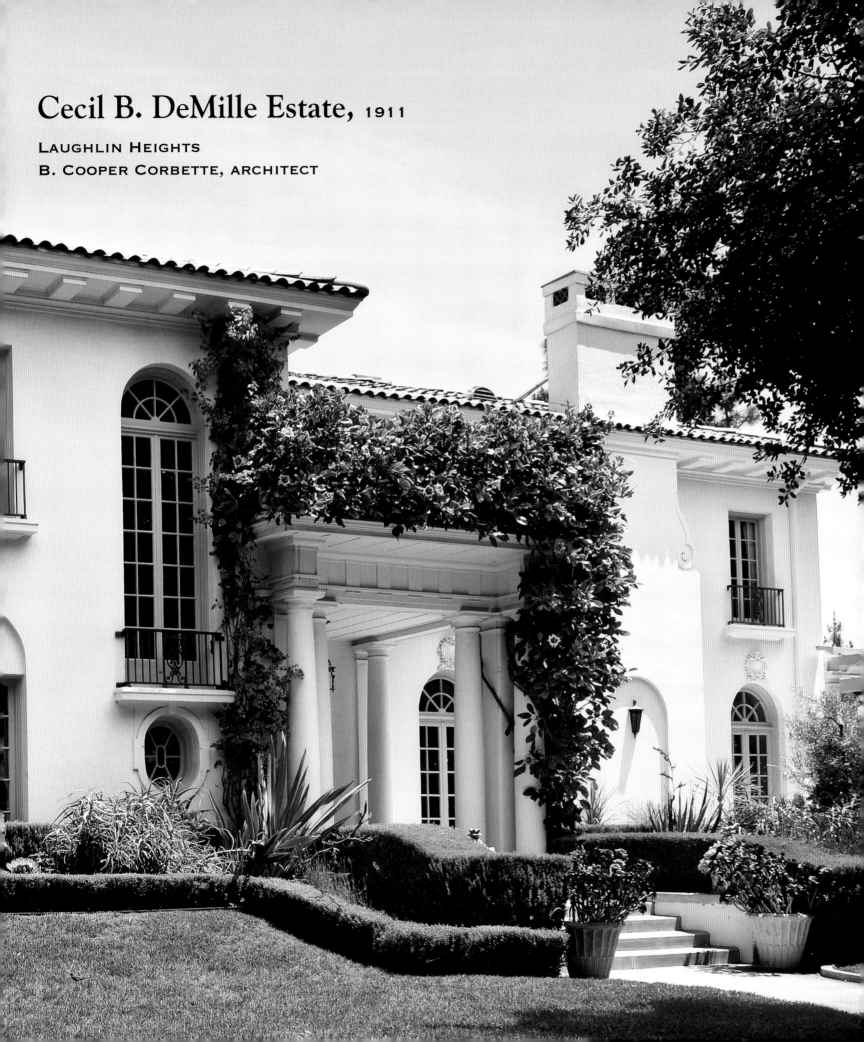

Cecil B. DeMille Estate, 1911

Laughlin Heights
B. Cooper Corbette, architect

ABOVE *The living room*

FACING PAGE *Artist Nicolas Africano's*
Drinking from a Bowl *fills an alcove at*
the bottom of the graceful staircase.

"See your favorite stars, committing your favorite sins" may have been a slogan used by Cecil B. DeMille, famed director for many of the lavish epics of Hollywood's Golden Age, but his home life and taste were more subdued than the line suggests. In private, DeMille was reportedly quiet and reserved, a sharp contrast to the pistol-packing megaphone persona by which he was known, and the home he bought from Los Angeles businessman C. F. Perry in 1916 stands in some contrast to the palatial homes later built by such peers as Buster Keaton and Douglas Fairbanks.

Located in the gated enclave of Laughlin Park, an early upper-class development hidden in the hills of Los Feliz, the house was built in 1911 by architect B. Cooper Corbette. Sober Italianate Revival in style, the residence crowns a two-acre grass knoll and has commanding views of the greater Los Angeles basin. From its approach, the house cuts a dignified silhouette against extensive greenery. Nearly 8,000 square feet, though with rooms of modest scale, the main house

feels as if it had been designed more for intimate family life than for entertaining, which apparently precisely fit the bill for DeMille.

In 1918, newlyweds Charlie Chaplin and his sixteen-year-old wife, Mildred Harris, purchased the house next door. The couple was divorced by 1920, and Chaplin sold the house to DeMille, who soon connected the two houses via a breezeway extending from an atrium, possibly designed by Julia Morgan. The old Chaplin House served as DeMille's office and screening room until his death in 1959. Both houses remained in the DeMille family for nearly three decades after that, preserved just as he had left them.

The current owners, avid architectural preservationists who have renovated a number of significant houses, found DeMille's estate in poor condition. The Chaplin House, designed by architect William J. Dodd, was literally crumbling and needed most immediate attention. The couple hired architects Brian Tichenor and Raun Thorp to restore the house. Over the next two years, the interior was dismantled and

LEFT *A view from the library past Philip Guston's* Suitcase, *into the fabled breezeway that once connected the DeMille house with Charlie Chaplin's, next door*

TOP *Another view of the library*

ABOVE *The dining room*

ABOVE *The Griffith Observatory peaks from the adjacent ridge in the distance*

RIGHT *The DeMille house sits perched on a knoll overlooking a pool and gardens designed by Brian Tichenor*

reassembled, preserving the famous Tudor living room and all the significant details. Eventually, the couple sold the Chaplin House, in order to devote their full attention to reviving the DeMille Estate. Tichenor and Thorp were called in again, this time to renovate the DeMille house and bring the landscape back to its former glory. The interiors now convey a sense of grandeur that was previously lacking. Ceilings were raised where possible. The servant's quarters were poached to make way for a bigger kitchen and library. Though the winding staircase and period details evoke the past, the art on the walls serve as a reminder that this nearly 100-year-old house is very much in the here and now. In remaking the garden, Tichenor looked to Florence Yoch, studying her plant lists for designs executed for other Hollywood moguls such as Jack Warner. He also designed a studio where DeMille's stables once stood and a new pool house.

Petitfils-Boos House, 1921

Hancock Park
Charles Plummer, architect

ABOVE *A detail of the stained glass panel over the main entryway*

FACING PAGE *A view from the library into the living room shows off the abundant decorative painting and detailed woodcarving found throughout the house.*

Charles Plummer was not the most prolific architect of the era, but two of his structures are included on the National Register of Historic Places. One is the Young's Market Company Building, built in 1924 and is now luxury lofts. The other is the house he designed for Walter Petitfils, who owned Petitfils Candy Store and Petitfils Restaurant.

This dazzling Italian Renaissance Revival house in Windsor Square may be the only single-family residence clad in Gladding McBean architectural terra-cotta. The Gladding McBean Company has been producing its famous glazed tile to sheath ornate civic and commercial buildings for 125 years. Their decorative wares are highly collectible. Plummer's choice of material follows the generous application of it on the exterior of Young's Market and other buildings downtown. The result produces a surreal effect that gives the impression it was just recently built. The glaze finish shows no natural sign of aging—which is ironically appropriate, considering the home's proximity to Hollywood.

The interiors have fine walnut paneling, stenciled beams, and impressive stained glass, but the real highlight is the murals by Anthony B. Heinsbergen. A Dutch immigrant who arrived in Los Angeles at 13, Heinsbergen attended Chouinard Art Institute and went on to do murals for the Roosevelt and Beverly Wilshire hotels;

TOP AND RIGHT *Living room and parlor*

RIGHT *The magnificent ceiling mural, painted by Anthony B. Heinsbergen*

FOLLOWING PAGES *The oval shaped ballroom and its wall of windows that face out to the garden*

ABOVE *The loggia with mosaic floor*

RIGHT *The formal dining room*

FOLLOWING PAGES *Little remained of the original garden designed by A. E. Hansen when the current owners took over. They redid the hardscaping and pool.*

then later, Los Angeles City Hall. Alexander Pantages, the theater mogul, commissioned him to do murals for his theater chain. This lead to national attention for Heinsbergen, and, by the end of his career, over 700 major commissions. His work is synonymous with the glamorous nightlife haunts of the 1930s.

The grounds had been altered from their original A. E. Hansen design, but the present owners have preserved the house faithfully.

Davis Estate, 1921

HANCOCK PARK

F. PIERPONT DAVIS AND WALTER S. DAVIS, ARCHITECTS

FACING PAGE *The richly carved front door framed by quoins in a sunburst pattern*

ABOVE *The blue room*

FOLLOWING PAGES *The heart of the house, the library*

Francis Pierpont and Walter Swindell Davis were the sons of Baltimore architect Frank E. Davis. The brothers followed in their father's footsteps and established their architectural practice in Los Angeles around 1915. They were pioneers in developing courtyard apartment housing based on Spanish and Italian designs. They embraced community dwellings planned around a common garden, and in 1916 published *Ideal Homes in Garden Communities* to promote their vision of community living. They also worked with the Olmsted brothers (sons of Frederick Law Olmsted, Sr., the designer of Central Park in New York) in Palos Verdes, south of Los Angeles.

Designed by F. Pierpont Davis for his wife, Gertrude Churchill, and family, this Italian Revival home warmly expresses the love Davis held for Mediterranean gardens and architecture. Completed in 1921, it is made of adobe brick and finished in a coffee stained stucco. Reminiscent of Villa Gamberaia near Florence, it is believed that the craftsmen who lived and worked on the site were brought from Italy for the job. The beautifully produced wrought iron, woodwork, and elaborate ceiling treatments exude a convincing authenticity. The walls are nearly three feet thick in places offering year round insulation, though the house opens to the garden at many points. Doors from the living room lead out to the loggia to the south and to the formal garden to the east. The dining room also opens up to the formal gardens to both the south and east.

The garden is comprised of four parts: a formal garden, a secret garden, woods (including a shade garden), and an orchard. A lap pool was incorporated into the orchard section. The garden, especially its formal section featuring vintage pomegranates, myrtle hedges, and old roses, has been faithfully maintained according to its original plan and has been accepted into the Smithsonian Institution Archives of American Gardens.

The current owners purchased the house from the Owen Churchill Trust, Churchill was Pierpont's brother-in-law. They have done little in the way of altering the house or its garden, remarkably situated on over an acre in the middle of the city. Floor-to-ceiling bookcases were added in the living room, and the kitchen was tastefully updated by architects Victoria Yust and Ian McIlvaine of Tierra, Sol y Mar.

TOP *The display table in the loggia came from Bullocks Wilshire's closing sale*

ABOVE *The kitchen underwent a sensitive update by Tierra, Sol y Mar architects.*

RIGHT *The dining room, with its wrap around groin vaulted ceiling*

TOP *A view from the loggia*

ABOVE *The formal geometry of the central garden seen from the second floor of the house*

RIGHT *A view from the garden. The balcony is split between open space off the master bedroom and enclosed space for a changing room.*

Churchill House, 1928

HANCOCK PARK
F. PIERPONT DAVIS AND WALTER S. DAVIS,
ARCHITECTS

ABOVE *A decorative mural ushers one to the entrance of the house.*

RIGHT *Devotional antiques add to the home's historical ambience.*

Pierpont Davis's brother-in-law, Owen Churchill, must have been taken with the architect's ability. He commissioned Davis to build a house for him and his wife on a lot not far from Davis's own.

Churchill was an avid yachtsman who competed in three consecutive Summer Olympics, winning gold in the 1932 Los Angeles games piloting his own *Angelita*, with his brother-in-law and architect on board to share the medal. Decades later he sailed the *Angelita* as a featured mascot in the 1984 Los Angeles games. Churchill made a name for himself in another way as well. Around 1936, while in Tahiti, he became intrigued by the crudely fashioned fins the locals used for diving. Noting the commercial possibilities, he brought the idea back with him and "invented" the Owen Churchill Swim Fin, which was a great success and is still popular today.

The Churchill House is another example of the architects' mastery of the Mediterranean style. From the street, it is less imposing than Pierpont Davis's own home, more Umbrian country than Florentine villa; and, whereas the Davis house has a formally centered front door framed in quoins, the Churchill's entrance is discretely placed in a pocket loggia on the south side of the forward wing. The house is set rather far into the lot, and the facade serves as the backdrop to the principal garden, which sits to the front of the house. The formal geometry of the garden centers on the Robert Graham sculpture, a

PRECEDING PAGES *The hall and dining room, with murals by Garth Benton*

RIGHT *The new wing's great room, designed by architect Lorenzo C. Tedesco*

FOLLOWING PAGES *Rear view of the house, with pool and newer wing to the right*

Duke Ellington memorial figure titled *Neith*, instead of a fountain, but incorporates many of the same elements, myrtle hedges and old roses, as Davis used in his own garden. The two stories of simple white stucco walls and low-pitched terra-cotta rooflines offer little hint of the rich decorative elements inside. The painted wood ceiling in the living room is elaborately carved and gives the room historical weight. The groin-vaulted ceilings in the main hall and dining room are similar to those at the Davis House and have been painted with Renaissance inspired murals by Garth Benton, a cousin of Thomas Hart Benton and one of the great American muralists. In a nod to the times, a narrow room reproducing the interior of the *Angelita* served as a speakeasy.

Grafted to the original structure, a new wing was added by architect Lorenzo C. Tedeso, and it successfully blends with the original parts of the house. The new sitting room, with its grand scale fireplace, has a beamed ceiling and copiously detailed stenciling. Also added was a paneled library that opens to a patio and pool.

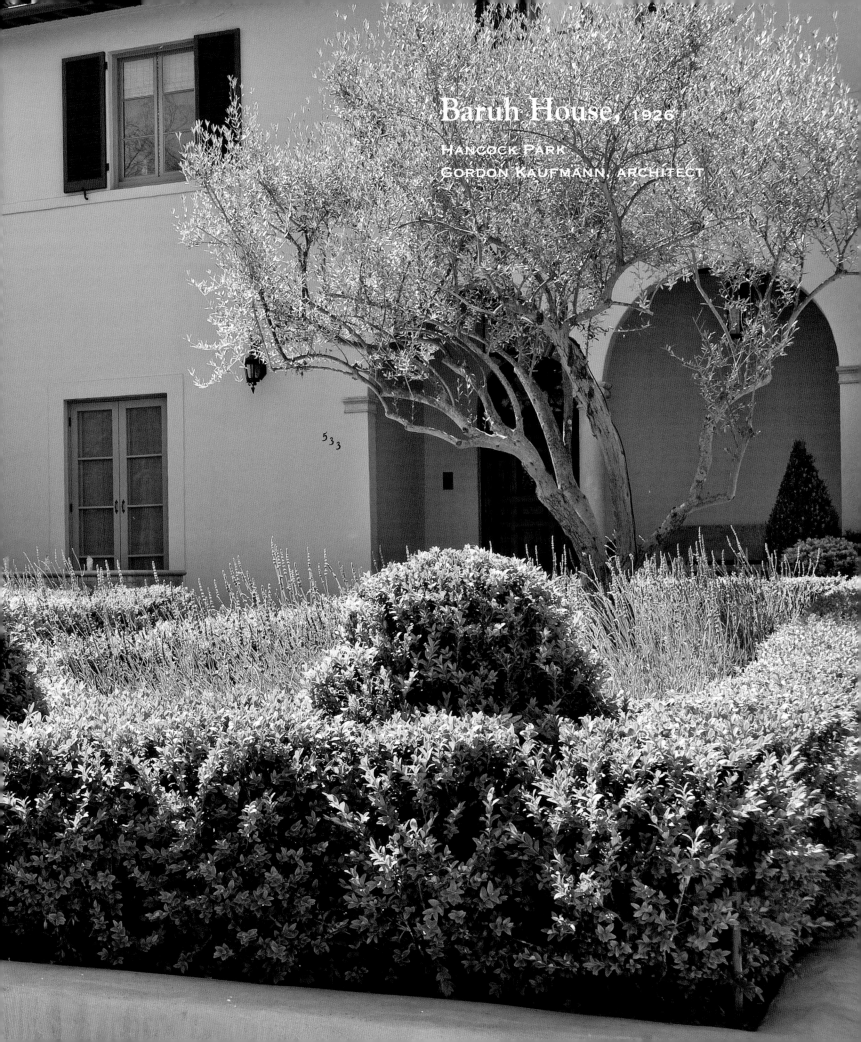

Baruh House, 1926

Hancock Park
Gordon Kaufmann, architect

ABOVE AND RIGHT *This logia and living room: clearly the ideal indoor–outdoor room.*

Architect Gordon Kaufmann made a name for himself as a partner in the firm Johnson, Kaufmann & Coate. After the firm dissolved, Roland Coate, Reginald Johnson, and Kaufmann continued to enjoy productive careers as individual practitioners. On his own, Kaufmann began building his signature Tuscan-inspired mansions in 1925, notably the Theodore Eisner House, which set the tone for many similar homes he would design.

The Baruh House, designed for Zellerbach Paper director J. Y. Baruh and his wife, Alma, in Hancock Park, is a fitting solution to the problem he saw in obtaining privacy in the city. The public face of the house has a flat and protective presence, with small shuttered windows and an understated corner entrance. The house guards its inner garden and the rooms that open to it. The inner spaces are voluminous and mostly spare in detail. The living room is enlivened by arched moldings and opens to a colonnade that runs the length of the garden. Above it, a second-story loggia provides an alternative to a porch. White plaster dominates the house inside and out except for the paneled formal dining room. As is often the case, the lot dictated the ultimate design. In this case, an L shape was employed over the more traditional Mediterranean courtyard, still achieving the effect of being transported somewhere tranquil, outside the city.

Kaufmann's later commissions were of a much grander scale. He designed, among other landmarks, the Los Angeles Times Building, Scripps College in Claremont (one of the most beautiful campuses anywhere), and Hoover Dam.

TOP *The kitchen and a glimpse of the family room*

ABOVE *Wrought iron banisters and hand-troweled arches typify the quiet glamour of the Mediterranean house.*

RIGHT *The details in the paneling of the dining room were hidden under decades of darkened lacquer until the current owners oversaw an arduous restoration.*

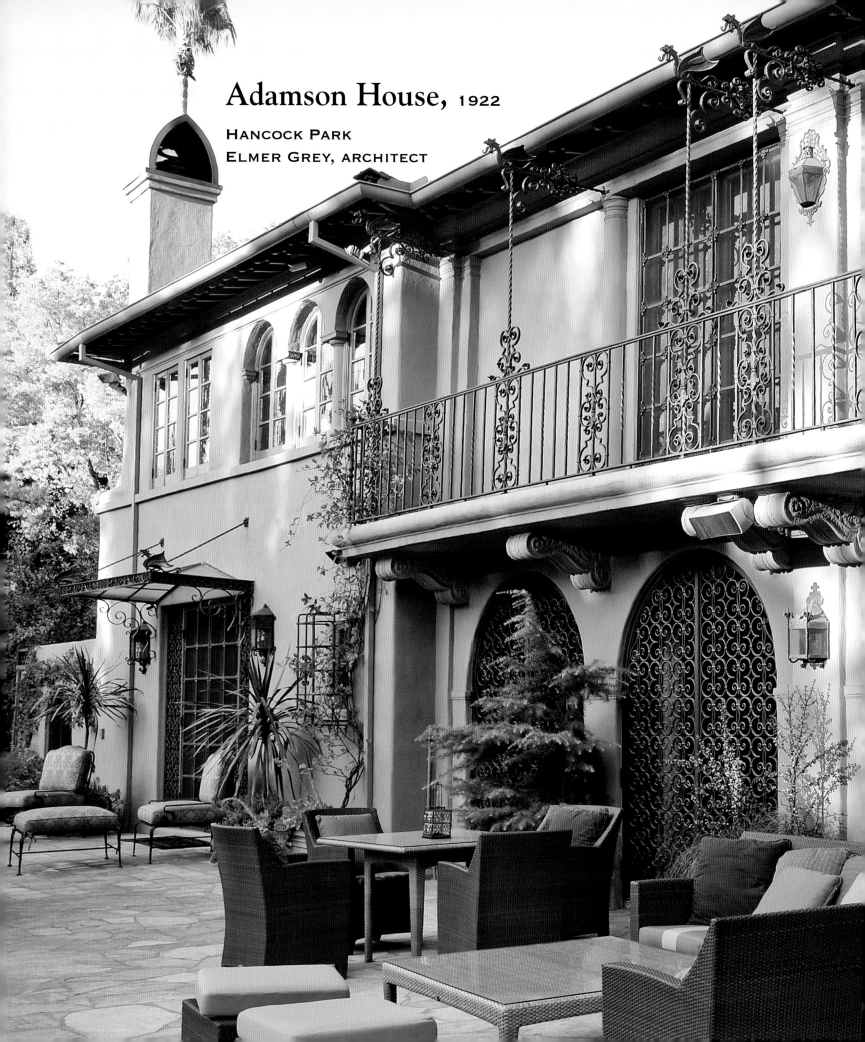

Adamson House, 1922

HANCOCK PARK
ELMER GREY, ARCHITECT

ABOVE *The fountain on the back patio. Also noteworthy are the terra-cotta columns on the guest house balcony.*

RIGHT *Garden architecture reminiscent of the Arts & Crafts movement sits perfectly at home in this garden oasis.*

Built for Merritt H. Adamson and his wife, Rhoda, this was the first of two well-known houses the couple would commission (the second, built in Malibu, follows). Designed by architect Elmer Grey in 1922, the house gradually evolved over the decades that followed. Significantly, Rhoda was the daughter of May Rindge, who, in 1923, founded the fabled Malibu Potteries not far from Vaquero Point where Merritt and his wife would build their beach house. A casualty of the Great Depression, Malibu Potteries closed in 1932, however, both this house and the one in Malibu owe much of their wonderful flavor to the company's expertly crafted tile.

The house would be a rather common example of Italian Mediterranean–styled residential architecture, but for its remarkable details. First, unlimited access to the Malibu Potteries greatly benefited this house. Like its sister at the beach, it boasts an interesting variety of tiles, notably on the floor of the sunroom and on the back patio fountain, with its unique blue starburst pattern. Second, the ironwork also offers some surprises, with Spanish and Italian patterns crowned in Celtic-style griffins. Decorative iron grille doors sheild all points of access downstairs to allow in the warm breeze without worry. In something of a design disconnect, a large wooden balcony was later imposed on the front of the house, giving the facade something of a Monterey feel from the street.

PRECEDING PAGES
Serving as a transition between indoor and out, this game room foreshadows the great things to come at the Adamson House in Malibu. The arched doors all open out to the garden.

LEFT *Looking down toward the landing of the finely crafted staircase*

FACING PAGE TOP *The dining room and the current owner's chinoiserie discovery*

FACING PAGE BOTTOM *Living room*

FOLLOWING PAGES *The pool area*

Over the years, the landscape has been reconfigured as portions of the once very large lot have been parceled off. What remains is still a beautiful garden of native plantings, a wisteria-covered trellis bordering the back of the lot, and a reproduction of the famous fountain in Malibu.

The current owners are passionate about restoring the house and in reestablishing a connection to its history. Restoration architects Mary Pickhardt, Bebe Johnson, and Ellen Geerer revived the house to its current picture-perfect state. As often becomes necessary with older homes, the kitchen was enlarged and is now adjoined by a large family room, while the former guest quarters above the garage have been converted into a screening room.

TOP AND ABOVE *Tiled fountains with the Pacific beyond*

RIGHT *A vignette where every detail is a testament to the profound ability of the human hand*

Location is almost everything. Vaquero Point, perched between the Malibu lagoon and the sandy shores of the Pacific Ocean, is as fine a spot as one will find to build a home. It is believed that the Native American Chumash valued the spot as well, having built a village here hundreds of years ago. At the time that May Rindge, the maven of Malibu, gave this site to her daughter and son-in-law, Malibu was essentially still her personal Eden. Having fended off everyone from bootleggers to the Southern Pacific Railroad, May was forced eventually to relent and make way for the Roosevelt (now

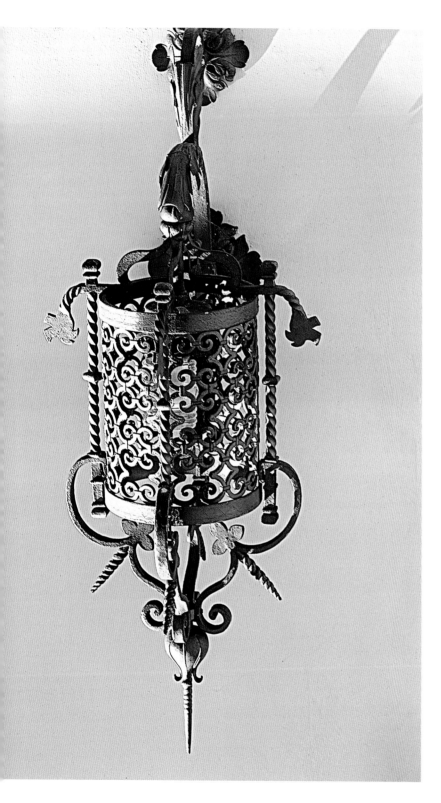

PRECEDING PAGES *A well-worn patina of smoke and age are a reminder of the home's storied history.*

LEFT *A wrought iron light fixture of elaborate intricacy*

FACING PAGE *The famous Persian rug in tile covers the floor of the loggia.*

Pacific Coast) Highway. It's hard to imagine the wonder of touring up the coast in 1926 and witnessing the marvel of the still unspoiled Santa Monica Mountains.

Merritt and Rhoda Adamson hired architect Stiles O. Clement of the venerable firm Morgan, Walls & Clement to design a house in the Spanish Colonial Revival style on this site. Clement, with his partners Octavius Morgan and John Walls, had a prolific office and as responsible for a long list of landmarks in Los Angeles, from the El Capitan and Mayan theaters to the Chapman Market and the regretfully demolished Atlantic Richfield Building. The firm did not build many houses.

The Adamsons ended up with a *relicario* to the tile arts, which had been elevated to a high form at the nearby Malibu Potteries May had founded, and one of the finest examples of Spanish Colonial Revival style to be found.

Today, the Adamson House is a National Historic Site and a jewel of the California State Parks system.

Morgan House, 1929

MIRACLE MILE
MORGAN, WALLS & CLEMENT, ARCHITECTS

LEFT *The hall between the foyer and the living room*

FACING PAGE *A mysterious stained glass window opens into the living room*

FOLLOWING PAGES *The one-and-a-half-story sunken living room with its impressive timber support*

At the time that the firm was building the Adamson House in Malibu, Octavius Morgan was planning his retirement. Stiles Clement designed this traditional Spanish courtyard-style house for his partner and friend in the Miracle Mile area of Los Angeles. Morgan, Walls & Clement had had a hand in designing some of the most elaborate picture palaces within the Broadway theater district, however, the over-the-top Churrigueresque and Art Deco styles for which they were well known seemed to have little influence on the design here.

Located on a corner and taking up two lots, the Morgan House is simple and pure. A flat tiled roof extends along the south-facing white stucco wall, which hides the home's main courtyard and wraps around the corner enveloping the deceivingly large sunken living room, allowing for a double height ceiling. The roof subtly pitches over the cavernous entryway and pitches again over the rest of the living wing. A single-story design, the house boasts a formal dining room, a library, the large living room, a master bedroom that opens up to its own private courtyard, and a full basement, rare in Southern California. There is also a four-car garage to boot. Other details, which encourage comparison with the Adamson Malibu house, include original hand-scored plaster ceilings found in the formal dining room and library, deep set windows designed to give the illusion of an adobe built structure, and numerous stenciled walls and ceilings that are present in both homes.

In recent years, architectural preservationist Brett Waterman was called in to work his magic, and he meticulously labored to restore the house. Thankfully, time was kind to the house, and it had not been fussed with excessively. Much of the restorers work involved removing layers of paint that hid refined craftsmanship, such as hand-carved doors on which hundreds of deep carved lines had been whitewashed, and releasing kitchen windows designed to disappear, rolling down into pockets in the wall to let the breeze in. Also noteworthy is the butter-like quality of the exterior plaster finish, which Waterman revisited more than once to get right.

PRECEDING PAGES LEFT *A view into the dining room, with its dyed and scored ceiling*

PRECEDING PAGES RIGHT *Original elaborate stenciling in the hall en route to the private wing of the house*

LEFT AND ABOVE *The main courtyard and outdoor fireplace*

Millard House, 1923

PASADENA

FRANK LLOYD WRIGHT, ARCHITECT

ABOVE AND RIGHT *Frank Lloyd Wright oversaw the site design. The pond is an invention.*

Mrs. Millard, widow of rare book dealer and Arts & Crafts movement proponent George Millard, was one of Frank Lloyd Wright's few return clients. Wright had built the couple a Prairie Style home in Highland Park, Illinois, in 1906, where they lived until moving to Pasadena, California, in 1914. After her husband's death in 1918, she took over the business. Alice Millard became well known for promoting the collecting of fine and rare books, and she counted among her clients such notables as William Andrews Clark, Templeton Crocker, Estelle Doheny, and Henry Huntington.

In the early 1920s, Alice purchased a lot in the Prospect Park section of Pasadena and hired Wright to build a house on the site. Wright being Wright, he decided he didn't like the site and suggested she purchase the lot just down the hill. Alice took his advice, but from then on did her best to reign him in. In the process, she risked everything she had to see the project through.

It is no secret that Frank Lloyd Wright didn't like Southern California. But, as it has for so many, the region provided a place for him

PRECEDING PAGES *The interior reflects the exterior in cascades of concrete block—like a beautiful ruin.*

LEFT AND ABOVE *Though a larger-than-life temple in silhouette, inside, the Millard House provides a human-scale experience, as felt here in a bedroom and on the staircase.*

to reinvent himself. Alice Millard's lot became a laboratory for Wright's first textile block experiments. Wright envisioned a structure built entirely of patterned blocks molded on-site from the earth he was building on. This approach is consistent with his love of natural materials but troublesome for builders (the first one quit), and subsequent preservationists.

Dubbed "La Miniatura," the Millard House is a temple of the earth reminiscent of pre-Columbian ruins. It is also an enduring Modernist icon set amongst a gracious collection of traditional revival homes, of which Wright had negative opinions. Though he is known to have disparaged the faux Mexican and Mission styles, one might wonder if adobe construction didn't influence his block technique. Critics at the

ABOVE *The kitchen*

RIGHT *The textile-block facade, seen from the approach, continues to be a revelation.*

time wondered why anyone would want to live in a house clad in such a lowly material, but this was the challenge Wright set for himself, and in the end he succeeded. Over time, the Millard House has come to be regarded by most as one of the twentieth century's iconic designs.

In 1927, Alice commissioned Lloyd Wright, Frank Lloyd Wright's son, to add a studio, which she later referred to as her "museum for books." Here she housed her library and held exhibitions celebrating the art of the book. Upon her death, friends purchased from her estate a collection of books on the history of books and gave them to the Huntington Library as The Alice and George Millard Collection Illustrating the Evolution of the Book.

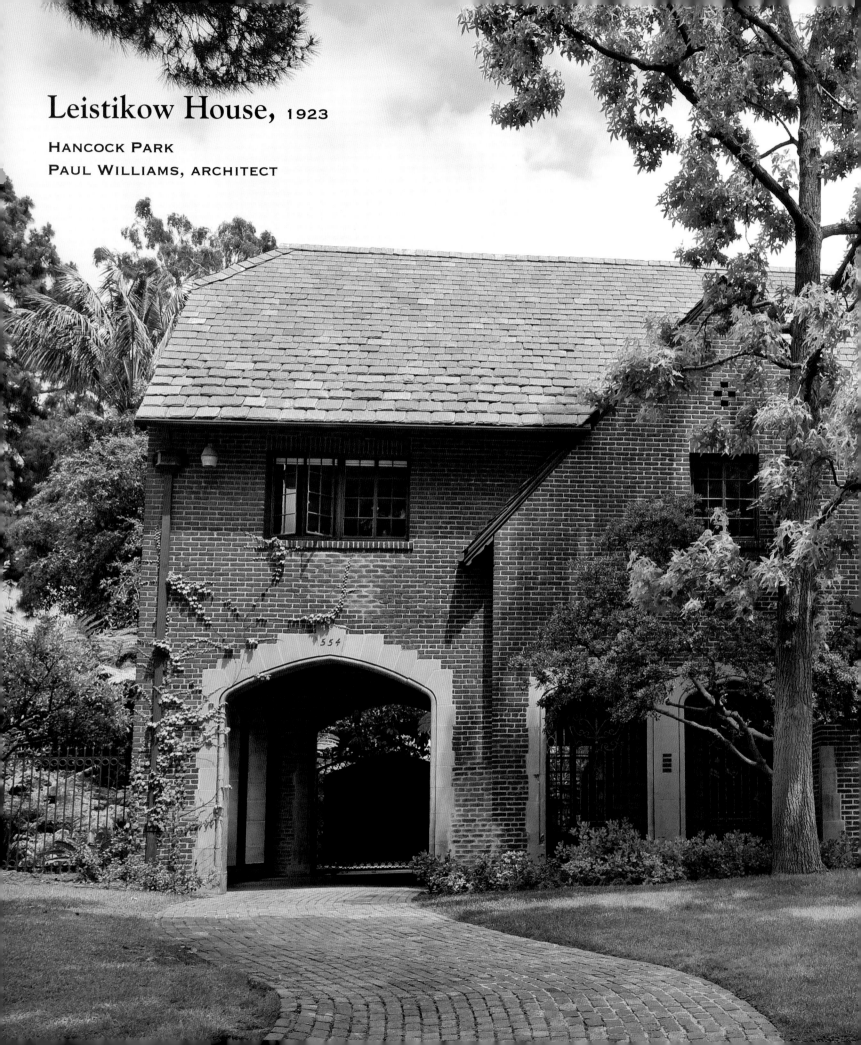

Leistikow House, 1923

Hancock Park
Paul Williams, architect

TOP *Stained glass detail with Frederick Leistikow's initials*

RIGHT *The landing foreshadow's Williams's penchant for a dramatic entry.*

In 1922, Paul Revere Williams opened an office in the Stock Exchange Building in downtown Los Angeles. He had spent the previous three years working for architect John C. Austin, and before that, Reginald Johnson. He was ready to go into practice for himself. With a commission referred by Austin to build a home in Hancock Park, a storied and history-making career was launched.

The odds of an African American born in Los Angeles in 1894 and orphaned by the age of four becoming one of the great American architects are incalculable, but such was the story of Paul Williams. His faith that the quality of his work would overcome the prejudices of his day is a testament to the strength of his character. His talent and fortitude won him many commissions from the elite of Los Angeles society and civic institutions. In addition to fine homes, he built schools and churches and left his mark on landmarks from the Beverly Hills Hotel to the Los Angeles International Airport. His legacy will likely be measured in equal parts for the high quality of work he left behind and the example he set for all who strive to overcome life's obstacles.

The bold English-style cottage he built for Frederick Leistikow in 1923 proved his ability to deftly adapt an antique regional style for a

RIGHT *The subtle pointed arch of the front door is echoed throughout the house.*

Modern city house. The stately brick edifice is balanced in mood by the staggered stair window. Inside, one is greeted by a trademark checkered floor and soaring stairway. The living room's lead and glass windows are accented with nautical-themed stained glass, and the FL monogram can be found on the Tudor mantel and in the ironwork. There is a richly paneled library and dining room as well as, between the living room and garden, a hint of the kind of outdoor room for which he later became well known.

FACING PAGE *A view of the staggered stair window with a nautical themed stained-glass motif. Images of exploration were a popular secular alternative to traditional religious themes often employed in stained glass. This is evident throughout the house.*

ABOVE *The living room*

FOLLOWING PAGES *Frederick Leistikow's initials are also found in various spots, including on the spark guard of the living room fireplace.*

Collins House, 1932

Hancock Park
Paul Williams, architect

ABOVE *The library with the hidden door ajar*

RIGHT *A view of the living room, with its shades of pinks, as approved by Williams*

Nearly a decade after completing the Leistikow House, Williams's first solo commission in Hancock Park, he wound up designing another house across the street that he would later deem one of his favorite houses. Unlike the decidedly English Leistikow House, the Collins House is classically French. This sophisticated exterior has similar elements to the interiors Williams would later do for Saks Fifth Avenue on Wilshire Boulevard and hints at a direction design was taking at that time.

Williams, along with architects such as John Woolf and James Dolena, at that time began to incorporate exaggerated Classical forms with Modern spaces. This "Hollywood Regency" style brought Classical opulence back into vogue, offering an alternative to the rigid Streamline Moderne style Hollywood had been championing for the last decade and a half.

In its life, the house has only known two families, and during their tenure it has changed very little. According to the current owner, Williams got wind of their intention to remodel in the late 1960s. Mr. Williams appeared at the door one day, and, to the owner's delight,

PRECEDING PAGES *Looking through the foyer to the dining room*

ABOVE *The elaborately designed speakeasy reminiscent of a nineteenth-century saloon*

RIGHT *The outdoor living room*

consulted on new colors for the living room and foyer. He also oversaw the kitchen update.

The signature sweeping staircase and the generously proportioned living and dining rooms weren't the only signature Williams touches. As with many of his homes, Williams added a secret space. In the library a hidden door disguised as a panel to th side of the fireplace opens to a fully appointed speakeasy. Upstairs, the bedrooms are more intimate in scale. As is often the case, the best room is outside, a brick patio with a fire pit and iron awning looking to the garden. A demonstration that Williams knew what it was really all about.

William Andrews Clark Memorial Library, 1926

WEST ADAMS DISTRICT
ROBERT FARQUHAR, ARCHITECT

ABOVE *An antique painted piano on the first floor of the library*

FACING PAGE *The music room*

This magnificent building is the heart of what once was the estate of William Andrews Clark, Jr., son of Montana senator William Andrews Clark. The senior Clark, one of the copper kings, made his fortune mining in the Southwest. His son, having benefited from this fortune, settled in the West Adams district of Los Angeles in 1910. Over the following decades, he acquired many adjoining lots until he owned the entire city block along West Adams Boulevard. On the property, he built a number of formal gardens and a private observatory.

Clark was an active philanthropist and supporter of the arts. He founded the Los Angeles Philharmonic in 1919. His true passion, however, was books. A devoted bibliophile, Clark's collection of English literature, dramatic works, and history was ever growing in these years. His precious volumes, kept at the time in the library of his mansion, were threatened once by fire, prompting him to plan a proper home for them.

He hired architect Robert Farquhar (who later served along with Pierpont Davis under Edwin Bergstrom and David Witmer as archi-

tect on the Pentagon in Washington, D.C.). Farquhar delivered an "English villa" in the tradition of Sir Christopher Wren. Perhaps in a nod to its environs, the library is built of a terra-cotta-colored brick. The facade features three ocular portals under low-pitched tile roofs on either side of the main entrance, giving the appearance of twins joined at the hip. This is further balanced by the symmetrical placement of a fountain and reflecting pool. The building was encompassed by a formal garden, now lost, designed by landscape architect Ralph Cornell.

By the time of his death, Clark had amassed a major collection of early English literature and history through 1800, the most complete holdings of Eric Gill and Oscar Wilde works and papers in the world, and an extensive selection of early California printed works. As was always his intention, the library was deeded to the University of California, Los Angeles, upon his death. It is open to scholars as well as to the public. In addition to housing the collection, periodically the library hosts "Chamber Music at the Clark" and recitals.

ABOVE *The richly detailed ceiling of the main library*

FACING PAGE *A view from the second story of the library*

ABOVE AND RIGHT *The display cases in the main hall are used for rotating exhibits. The walls and floor are marble. The murals were executed by artist Allyn Cox.*

Griffith House, 1929

HANCOCK PARK
JONATHAN RING, ARCHITECT

ABOVE *Front facade*

FACING PAGE *The dramatic curved stairway from the entry foyer*

As the story goes, Mary Griffith, a native San Franciscan, survived the great earthquake and fire of 1906. She moved to Southern California, as many did, to escape the demolished Bay Area. The terror of that experience must have resurfaced periodically as smaller quakes occurred in and around Los Angeles. 1920 was a particularly active year, with over 100 such quakes recorded, but far worse was the devastating 1925 Santa Barbara earthquake and subsequent fire that practically destroyed that city. It is noteworthy that this resulted in the city abandoning its penchant for wooden Victorian architecture and rebuilding in the far sturdier Spanish Colonial style for which it is now famous. Perhaps taking these events as a cue, Ms. Griffith decided to build a house that she could count on to survive such a catastrophe.

It is possible that while staying at San Diego's famous Hotel Del Coronado she became acquainted with southern architect Jonathan Ring. Ring was doing a renovation at the hotel in 1928. In any event, Ring was hired to build her fortress on a lot facing the greens of the Wilshire Country Club in Hancock Park.

The house is purported to have cost $110,000 to build. Much of this went into the reenforcement of the structure, especially its huge basement foundation of poured concrete. Having now gone through substantial earthquakes without issue since construction, it seems clear that Griffith's money was well spent.

This distinguished Georgian has many of the elements of the great American Colonial Revival houses of the south. Though it doesn't sit on a 300-acre seat, the idyllic borrowed view gives the impression that it does. The impressive aedicular door surround supports a complementary Classical design around the stair window. Inside, one immediately comes upon a curving staircase that soars fluidly to the second floor. The paneling, elaborate mantels, and ceiling plasterwork throughout are all original. The walls of the formal dining room are graced with Zuber wallpaper.

In recent years, Marc Appleton & Associates reworked the driveway, built a porte-cochere, and designed a whole new landscape plan and pool area. They also converted the old garage into the recreation room.

TOP *View of the living room and kitchen. The gilt acanthus molding is repeated in the sitting and dining rooms.*

RIGHT *The walls of the dining room are graced with Zuber wallpaper.*

FOLLOWING PAGES *Doors from the living room lead out to a large awning-covered patio suitable for entertaining in any season.*

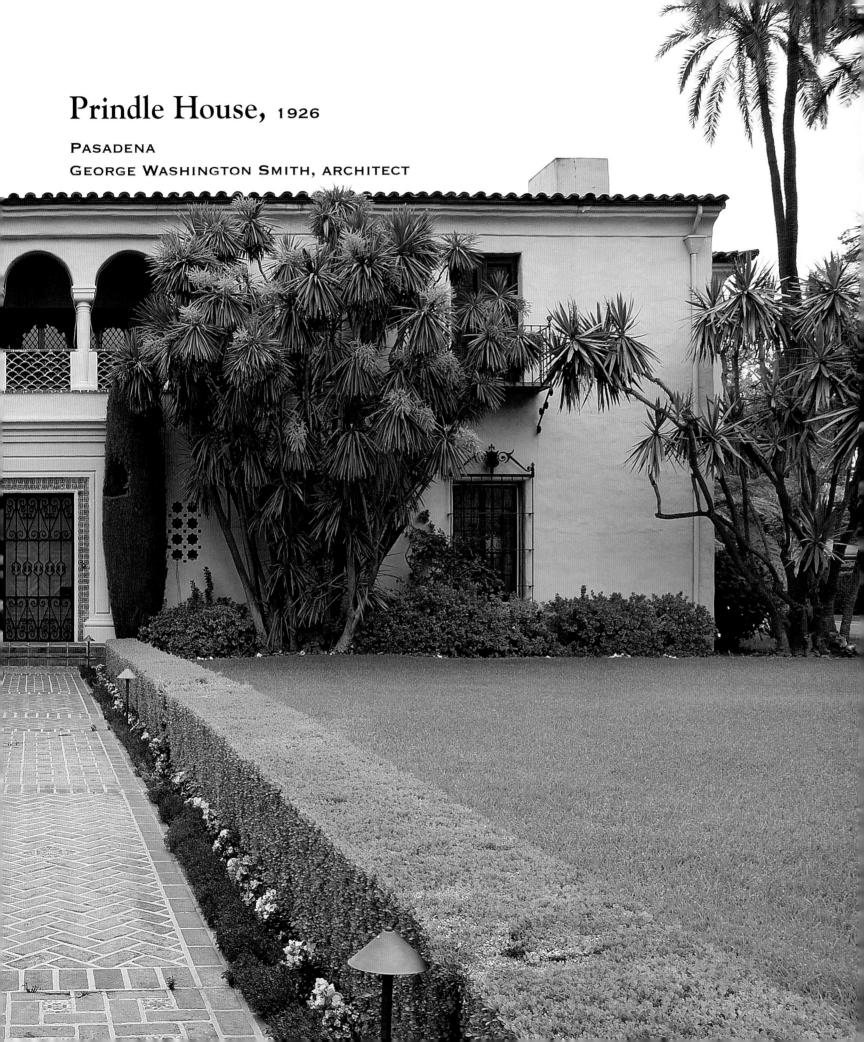

Prindle House, 1926

PASADENA
GEORGE WASHINGTON SMITH, ARCHITECT

ABOVE *A bench built of antique brick and tile*

FACING PAGE *This stunning entryway shows off some of the reclaimed antique materials integrated into the architecture.*

FOLLOWING PAGES *The dining room is the same today as it was in the 1920s. Note the rosettes incorporated into the floor tile pattern.*

The timeless living room is anchored by a monumental hooded chimneypiece.

It is rare today to encounter a home of this period that has not been tampered with. Unsympathetic renovations have degraded the quality of many of the greats. This house, designed by George Washington Smith, has not suffered such indignity. Still in the same family it was designed for three generations ago, it stands as a monument to the timelessness of superb design.

An artist turned architect, George Washington Smith settled in the Santa Barbara suburb of Montecito around 1917. He had some architectural training from Harvard, which he put to use in building a house and studio for himself inspired by the Andalusian farmhouses he saw while living in Europe. An appropriate choice it would seem, considering the similar Mediterranean climates, but during this period Queen Anne and the Victorians still reigned in California. Smith's paintings didn't sell at the time, but people loved his house—and, understanding something fundamental about his talents, he changed professions. By the time of his death in 1930, Smith, the father of the Spanish Colonial Revival style, had

defined the architectural look of Southern California and left us such landmarks as Casa del Herrero and the Lobero Theater in Santa Barbara.

The Prindle House was built late in the architect's career, and it was with the close involvement of the client that the final result was achieved. Together, client and architect went on buying trips to Italy, Spain, and Morocco in search of authentic elements to incorporate into the house. They returned with antique tile, light fixtures, iron, furniture, and doors, all of which were custom fit into the house. The result is a dramatic Spanish Colonial Revival house built around a courtyard. Beyond an Islamic star-shaped fountain, antique mosque doors open from the courtyard into a garden almost certainly inspired by those at Granada. The antique Spanish and Italian furniture, decorative art, tapestries, and paintings remain in situ. Over the decades, a patina of age has shaded the house, highlighting its historical authenticity. Today, it remains a remarkable home in a neighborhood blessed with architectural riches.

FACING PAGE *The grand foyer is filled with antique treasures from all over the world, including large Moroccan Kasbah lanterns, a fine Muslim prayer screen, a Japanese trunk, and French torchères. The green finials on the banister are blown glass.*

ABOVE *More heirlooms line the hall.*

FOLLOWING PAGE LEFT *Doors from an old mosque open to the gardens.*

FOLLOWING PAGE TOP RIGHT
The central courtyard with its striking sunken star fountain

FOLLOWING PAGE BOTTOM RIGHT
A view of the loggia

Lamb House, 1927

HANCOCK PARK
LESTER G. SCHERER, ARCHITECT

ABOVE *The front doorway framed by a decorative concrete frieze*

RIGHT *The living room with its great spans of timber largely unobtainable today*

The realization of Lucile Mead Lamb's house was a family affair. Her father, Willis Howard Mead, a self-made man in the timber industry and later head of the Whiting-Mead building supply company, seemed to have relished the adventure of letting his little girl oversee the design of her eventual dream house. Praise was reaped on the house in local newspapers when it was completed and it continues today. Both the folly of a twelve-year-old girl and the masterpiece of a little-known architect, the Lamb House (also known as La Casa de las Campañas) remains the standard by which great Spanish Colonial homes are measured.

Perhaps it was arduous for the hired architect, Lester Scherer, to work under these conditions. It may be, however, that he was inspired by the bright-eyed girl and her designs. Willis Mead managed the project and was generous, with both financing and excellent building materials, including now-untouchable twenty-foot spans of California redwood. Between father, daughter, and a twenty-two-year-old cousin who supervised two hired contractors—one for plaster and travertine, the other for wrought iron—a great home was built.

La Casa de las Campañas has the presence of a noble caballero, a knight of old Spain. Its seemingly impenetrable facade and recessed bell tower possess an air of historical purity. The iron, wrought on site, the tile choices, the quality woodwork, and travertine all give the house weight and permanence.

TOP *The breakfast room*

ABOVE *The billiard room*

RIGHT *A view from sitting room.
The archway leads back to the
game room, while the bookshelf-
door opens to the bar.*

TOP *A sitting area. The leaded glass softens the view to the gardens.*

ABOVE *A view of the reclaimed conservatory, now used for dining*

RIGHT *Detail of the stained glass mural*

The current owner, who purchased the home and its contents from the Lamb estate, is an ardent preservationist. He has not only reworked the interiors with the help of interior designer Rich Assenberg, utilizing the best of the Lamb collection, but he has also tracked down items related to the Mead family and repatriated those items throughout the house.

A Los Angeles Cultural Heritage site, it was restored by architects Milofsky & Michali and landscape architect Thomas Cox.

TOP *A detail of a tile mural with noteworthy foliage*

ABOVE *The Bell tower looms like an old soul.*

RIGHT *The pool area and its shaded retreat beyond*

Gosser House, 1928

HANCOCK PARK
MILTON J. BLACK, ARCHITECT

ABOVE *Painted balusters and exaggerated cantilevers supporting a second floor extension*

RIGHT *A variety of tropicals and succulents gathered at the entrance. Note the tile panels in the door.*

Milton J. Black is known as the architect of many notable Streamline Moderne houses and apartment buildings in Los Angeles. Along with William Kesling, they typified the clean-line look of 1930s Southern California. Perhaps he arrived at this style having exhausted every Spanish twist and turn he could muster to complete the Gosser House in 1928.

This structure of plaster, clay, and tile is a standout in the neighborhood for its use of color. To this day, Mission white is the standard finish for all things Mediterranean. Although such contemporaries as Everett Babcock and Sylvanous Marston did encourage their clients to experiment with color, Milton Black succeeded in getting his to celebrate its potential.

The peach patina now evident is a supposed match to the original. In windows, over doors, and running under banisters, hundreds of intricately tooled and hand-painted balusters accent the house. Doors are framed in and inlaid with antique tile. The roof tiles are larger than ordinarily seen and seem to have been produced on-site using the traditional method of a worker shaping the still-wet clay over his thigh, and in this case, using his fingers to create striations on the surface. On close examination many even have clearly visible fingerprints.

ABOVE *The decorative iron railing climbs the elaborately detailed rotunda*

RIGHT *Painted beams and plastered arches combine to make a dramatic ceiling in the living room.*

ABOVE *Hand-wrought terra-cotta roof tiles*

RIGHT *A view of the main courtyard*

The interior is voluminous and carpeted in red cement tile. The grand staircase, accented with more decorative tile, winds up a mammoth rotunda, from which hangs a large antique casbah lantern. A thick L-shaped colonnade of arches hugs the large inner courtyard. The lush landscaping, from roses, ferns, and cactus, to bougainvillea, gardenias, and palms, champions the fact that nearly anything will grow in this desert in denial that is Los Angeles.

Earl Estate, 1925

La Cañada-Flintridge

Everett Babcock, Architect

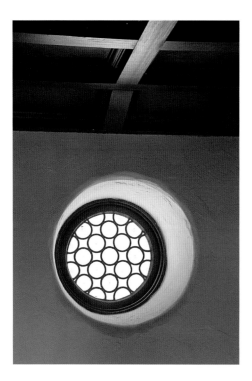

ABOVE *An ocular window*

RIGHT *Arches in plaster and shadow looking through the foyer*

La Cañada Flintridge, a bucolic community nestled in the San Gabriel Mountains in northern Los Angeles County, is home to a large concentration of great houses by the likes of architects Myron Hunt, Paul R. Williams, and others. Though Everett Babcock didn't live long enough to make a bigger name for himself, he left behind a number of beautifully produced homes in the area on par with the great architects of his time.

Originally from New York, Babcock practiced in Washington State before moving to Pasadena with his wife around 1923. His first job upon arriving was in Wallace Neff's office where he likely refined his talent for designing in the style of the Spanish Colonial Revival.

About 1925, Babcock established his own practice. One of his first solo commissions was for William Jarvis Earl, son of Alta Canyada's founder, Edwin T. Earl. Babcock seized the opportunity to build a house that possibly served as a model for others designed for the tract. With its undulating plaster, hipped and gabled clay tile roof, deep set windows and doors, the Earl House has all the elements of a quintessential Spanish California transplant. Babcock added some unique touches of his own. In a clever solution to adapting to the sloped lot, an arched colonnade steps down alongside the garden and detailed tooling of the protruding timber beams over the front door add drama to the approach.

PRECEDING PAGES *A view of the living room with recessed bookcases on either side of the fireplace*

ABOVE AND RIGHT *The master suite with its tiled bath and antique Spanish furnishings.*

It seems this extremely well-built house never fell into disrepair over the years. Understandably, though, a house sometimes has to be updated to meet the needs of today's family. Thankfully there are architects like Michael Burch and Diane Wilk who know how to take a house like this, add a new kitchen, family room, master suite, and spa, while leaving the impression that everything is as it always was. The layers of paint removed from the great timber ceiling of the living room are a reminder to all historic homeowners to think before you act. Burch's artistic use of tile, colored glass, and the addition of fountains fit with the design trends of the day and would likely have met with Babcock's approval.

TOP AND ABOVE *Architect Michael Burch had to reconfigure the approach to the house. A fountain now greets one at the entrance. He also enlivened parts of the house with generous use of tile.*

RIGHT *A colonnade dances down the sloped lot*

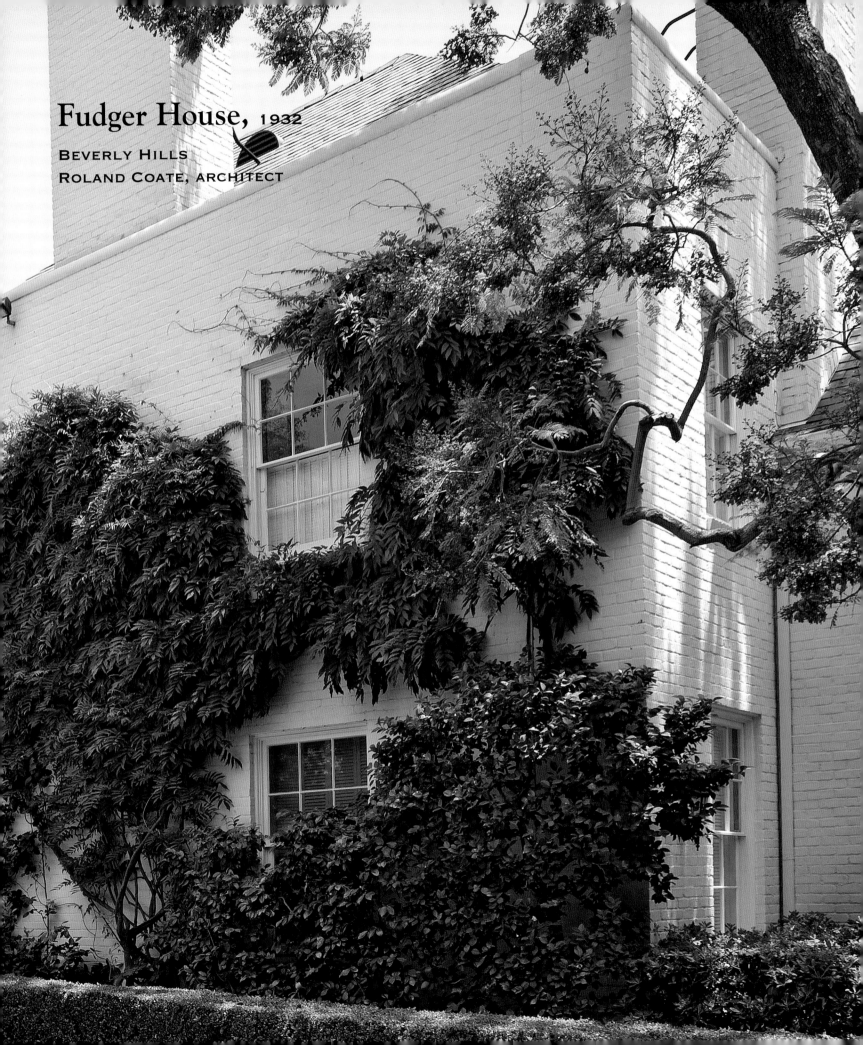

Fudger House, 1932

BEVERLY HILLS
ROLAND COATE, ARCHITECT

I n 1932, Roland Coate completed what was his second home for Mrs. Richard Fudger. Located in Beverly Hills not far from the Beverly Hills Hotel, this house combines elements of French Regency and Georgian Revival architecture. It is a departure from the first house he designed for the Fudgers, a well-known Spanish-style house in Hancock Park later owned by Howard Hughes. For the new house, Coate created a restrained space that gracefully blends the symmetrical elements of the Georgian style and echoes of French Colonial influence. The subtle use of detail throughout the house achieves a balance between the gracious and the comfortable. In 1933, the house received first prize in the sixth annual House Beautiful Small House Competition, Western Division, and the American Institute of Architects, in their 1939 annual, referred to the house as "… one of the finest examples of the Georgian and French influences," further praising it as being, "noteworthy for its beautiful proportions …"

The landscaping, designed by Florence Yoch and Lucile Council, is less restrained. The wisterias envelope a good portion of the facade, relaxing the house's otherwise austere formal face, and old roses complement the back garden and frame the pool.

In 1939, Fudger sold the house to director Rowland V. Lee, who made many films, including such well-known classics as *The Three Musketeers*, *The Count of Monte Cristo*, *The Guilty Generation*, *Son of Frankenstein*, and *The Bridge of San Luis Rey*. In 1940, Lee sold the house to Lewis Milestone, a very famous director who won two Academy Awards for directing: one for *Two Arabian Nights* and a second for *All Quiet on the Western Front*. He also directed *Front Page*, *Of Mice and Men*, *Ocean's Eleven* (1960), and *Mutiny on the Bounty* (1962). In 1952, Milestone sold the house to actor Danny Kaye, beloved by many for work in such movies as *White Christmas* and *The Court Jester*. He lived in the house until his death in 1987. Kaye was an avid chef, particularly Chinese fare, and he built a "Chinese kitchen" off the main kitchen and equipped it with a stove designed to accommodate three woks and a special oven for making Peking duck. He also encouraged his more artistically inclined guests to leave their mark on a wall in what was then the music room. Today, the wall remains as it was left, including caricatures of Kaye and some highball-inspired graffiti.

The current owners have faithfully preserved the house and it has adapted well to their lifestyle. Hardly a time capsule, a beautiful mix of antique English furniture and porcelain, Art Deco and modernist pieces, as well as an impressive collection of contemporary art are all at home here.

PRECEDING PAGES *Another view of the living room. The lamps on either side of the fireplace were fabricated by Billy Haines for the Deutch House in Beverly Hills in the late 1950s and incorporate Armand Albert Rateau birds.*

LEFT *A view of the dining room*

TOP *Danny Kaye's "Chinese kitchen"*

ABOVE *The grafittied wall of the old music room featuring drawings of Kaye by friends*

FOLLOWING PAGES *The pool, designed by William Pereira, is right at home in the lovely Florence Yoch garden.*

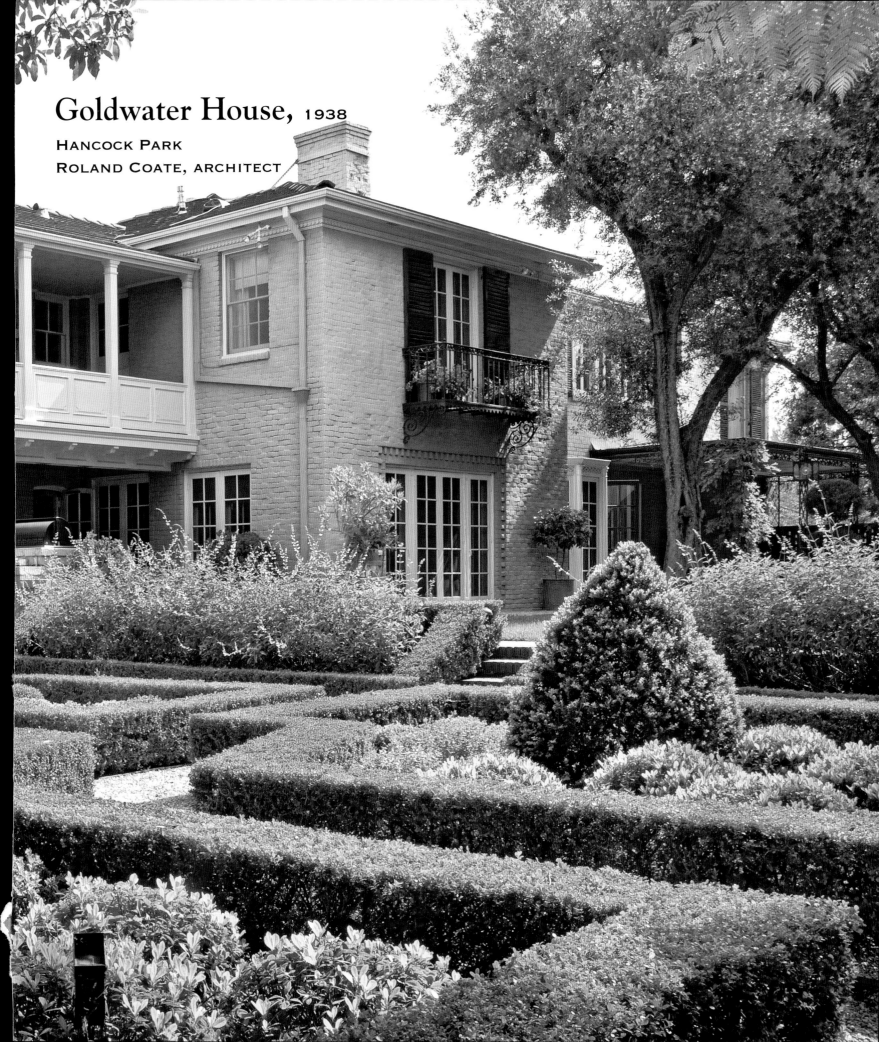

Goldwater House, 1938

HANCOCK PARK
ROLAND COATE, ARCHITECT

LEFT *The patio, ideal for outdoor dining. The fireplace was designed by Virgil McDowell.*

TOP *The formal entry nestled into a corner of the otherwise unassuming facade*

ompleted in 1938 by Roland Coate for A. F. Garrett, who never lived in the house and about whom little is known, it is the subsequent owners, Lemuel Goldwater and his wife Hortense, upon whom the house story turns. Descended from a pioneer family of Jewish descent whose Old West roots reach back at least as far as Arizona in the 1860s, Goldwater and his wife made the house their home for many years, and Goldwater lived there until his death in 1942.

Early on, Lemuel Goldwater had worked for one of the original garment factories in the now-huge Los Angeles garment district, successfully "graduating" to build and own a factory of his own. His company successfully made sportswear, and the building on East 12th Street is still in use today. In later life a philanthropist, Goldwater gave back much to the community and at one time sat on the founding board of Cedars of Lebanon, now Cedars-Sinai Medical Center.

This unique property in the Hancock Park neighborhood of Los Angeles. sits sideways on a quiet street not far from the La Brea Tar Pits. The unimposing facade features a signature Coate wrought-iron awning over a traditional Georgian-style entry, situated off a corner of the house. The understated view from the street is deceiving. Upon entering the foyer, the house unfolds into generously proportioned rooms, most of which flow seamlessly into the garden. Here, Coate's

thoughtful marriage of house and garden creates a perfect environment for entertaining, which the current owners do year-round, thanks to Edenic Southern California weather. The garden, designed by renowned landscape architect A. E. Hansen, has been faithfully restored and was recently accepted into the Smithsonian Institution Archives of American Gardens as an exemplar of its kind. Hansen was as attuned to the merging of the indoor-outdoor environments as was Coate. His design plays like a conversation between house and garden. The patio serves as the outdoor living room. Boxwood hedges frame intersecting paths that terrace down to a small formal garden and fountain. Architect Virgil McDowell, who did some of the home's interior renovation, designed the outdoor brick fireplace, which seamlessly blends with the existing wall. Thanks to color consultant Scott Flax, the perfect gray was selected to accentuate the white molding details and black shutters.

The interiors have undergone a few sensitive updates but remain largely as Coate designed them. The only major exception being the dining room, where artist David Wiseman has created a stunning Neobaroque garden scene in porcelain on the ceiling. Rodman Primack introduced the couple to the artists and helped assemble the stand out collection, including the Lalanne sculpture in the garden.

ABOVE AND TOP *The paneled library and living room*

RIGHT *The dining room, with paintings by Tony de los Reyes on the walls and a neo-Baroque garden scene in porcelain by David Wiseman on the ceiling*

The collage panels in the powder room are by artist Scott Calhoun. A close inspection reveals that the heads of the butterflies are photos of family friends. Other photos are woven into the pictures as well.

Bibliography

Ames, Meriam. *Rancho Santa Fe: A California Village*. San Diego, CA: Rancho Santa Fe Historical Society, 1995.

Appleton, Marc. *George Washington Smith: An Architect's Scrapbook*. Los Angeles, CA: Tailwater Press, 2001.

Appleton, Marc, and Melba Levick. *California Mediterranean*. New York: Rizzoli, 2007.

Banham, Reyner. *Los Angeles: The Architecture of Four Ecologies*. Berkeley, CA: University of California, 1971.

Baxter Art Gallery. *Caltech, 1910–1950: An Urban Architecture for Southern California*. Pasadena, CA: Caltech, 1983.

Baxter Art Gallery. *Myron Hunt, 1868–1952. The Search for Regional Architecture*. Santa Monica, CA: Hennessey & Ingalls, 1984.

Bonino, MaryAnn. *The Doheny Mansion: A Biography of a Home*. Los Angeles, CA: Edizioni Casa Animata, 2008.

Bricker, Lauren Weiss. *Johnson, Kaufmann, Coate: Partners in the California Style*. Claremont, CA: Scripps College, 1992.

Brownlow, Kevin, and John Kobal. *Hollywood: The Pioneers*. New York: Knopf, 1979.

Byne, Arthur, and Mildred Stapley. *Majorcan Houses and Gardens: A Spanish Island in the Mediterranean*. New York: William Helburn, 1928.

———. *Spanish Interiors and Furniture*. New York: William Helburn, 1925.

———. *Spanish Gardens and Patios*. Philadelphia, PA: J. B. Lippincott, 1924.

———. *Spanish Ironwork*. New York: Hispanic Society, 1915.

Clark, Robert Judson, and Thomas Hines. *Los Angeles Transfer: Architecture in Southern California 1880–1980*. Los Angeles, CA: Willam Andrews Clark Memorial Library, 1983.

Dailey, Victoria, Natalie Shivers, and Michael Dawson. *LA's Early Moderns: Art/Architecture/Photography*. Los Angeles, CA: Balcony, 2003.

Danky, James P., and Wayne A. Weigand, eds. *Women in Print: Essays on the Print Culture of American Women from the 19th & 20th Centuries*. Madison: University of Wisconsin, 2006.

Davis, Margaret Leslie. *Dark Side of Fortune: Triumph and Scandal in the Life of Oil Tycoon Edward L. Doheny*. Berkeley, CA: University of California, 1998.

———. *Bullocks Wilshire*. Los Angeles: Balcony Press, 1996.

———. *Rivers in the Desert: William Mulholland and the Inventing of Los Angeles*. New York: Harper Collins, 1993.

Davis, Walter S., and F. Pierpont Davis. *Ideal Homes in Garden Communities*. New York: McBride, 1916.

DeLyster, Dydia. *Ramona Memories: Tourism and the Shaping of Southern California*. Minneapolis: University of Minnesota, 2005.

Deverell, William. *Whitewashed Adobe: The Rise of Los Angeles and the Remaking of its Mexican Past*. Berkeley, CA: University of California, 2004.

Deverell, William, and Greg Hise. *Land of Sunshine: An Environmental History of Los Angeles*. Pittsburgh, PA: University of Pittsburg, 2005.

Eerdmas, Emily Evans. *Regency Redux: High Style Interiors, Napoleonic, Classical Moderne, and Hollywood Regency*. New York: Rizzoli, 2008.

Gebhard, David, and Robert Winter. *1868–1968, Architecture in California*. Santa Barbara, CA: University of California, Santa Barbara, 1968.

———. *A Guide to Architecture in Los Angeles and Southern California*. Layton, UT: Peregrine Smith, 1977.

———. *Los Angeles: An Architectural Guide*. Salt Lake City, UT: Gibbs Smith, 1994.

Gebhard, Patricia. *George Washington Smith: Architect of the Spanish-Colonial Revival*. Layton, UT: Gibbs Smith, 2005.

Goodhue, Bertram Grosvenor. *The Architecture and the Gardens of the San Diego Exposition*. Panama-California International Exposition. San Francisco, CA: Elder, 1916.

Graves, J. A. *My Seventy Years in California*. Los Angeles, CA: Times Mirror, 1927.

Greenberg, David, and Kathryn Smith. *Malibu Tile*. Los Angeles, CA: Craft and Folk Art Museum, 1980.

Hancock, Ralph. *Fabulous Boulevard*. New York: Funk & Wagnalls, 1949.

Hannaford, Donald R., and Revel Edwards. *Spanish Colonial or Adobe Architecture of California*. New York: Architectural Book Publishing Co., 1931.

Hansen, A. E., David Gebhard, and Shiela Lynds. *An Arcadian Landscape. The California Gardens of A. E. Hanson*. Santa Monica, CA: Hennessey + Ingalls, 1985.

Heimann, Jim. *Los Angeles, Portrait of a City*. Los Angeles, CA. Taschen, 2010.

Hess, Alan. *Rancho Deluxe: Rustic Dreams and Real Western Living*. San Francisco, CA: Chronicle Books, 2000.

Hudson, Karen. *Paul R. Williams: A Legacy of Style*. New York: Rizzoli, 1993.

Hunter, Paul Robinson, and Walter L. Reichardt. *Residential Architecture in Southern California*. AIA, 1939. Santa Monica, CA: Hennessey & Ingalls, reprinted, 1998.

Kanner, Diane. *Wallace Neff and the Grand Houses of the Golden State*. New York: Monacelli, 2005.

Lamb, Lucile Mead. ". . .Tells of Her Adventures in Homebuilding." Los Angeles: Themus, Zeta Tau Alpha, 1929.

Lewis, Oscar. *The Big Four: The Story of Huntington, Stanford, Hopkins, and Crocker and the Building of the Central Pacific*. New York: Knopf, 1945.

Lockwood, Charles. *Dream Palaces: Hollywood at Home*. New York: Viking, 1981.

Marcus, Clare Cooper. *House as a Mirror of Self: Exploring the Deeper Meaning of Home*. Berkeley, CA: Conari Press, 1995.

Marschner, Janice. *California 1850: A Snapshot in Time*. Sacramento, CA: Coleman Ranch Press, 2000.

McMillian, Elizabeth. *California Colonial: The Spanish and Rancho Revival Styles* (Schiffer Design Book). Atglen, PA: Schiffer Publishing, 2002.

McMillian, Elizabeth, and Melba Levick. *Casa California: Spanish-Style Houses from Santa Barbara to San Clemente*. New York: Rizzoli, 1996.

McWilliams, Carey. *Southern California Country*. Duell, Sloan & Pearce, 1946. Reprinted as *Southern California: An Island on the Land*. Santa Barbara, CA: Gibbs Smith, 1973.

Moore, Charles, Gerald Allen, and Donlyn Lyndon. *The Place of Houses*. Berkeley, CA: University of California, 2000.

Mullgardt, Louis Christian. *The Architecture and Landscape Gardening of the Exposition*. Panama-Pacific International Exposition. San Francisco: Elder, 1915.

Mulholland, Catherine. *William Mulholland and the Rise of Los Angeles*. Berkeley, CA; University of California, 2000.

Neff, Jr., Wallace (ed.), David Gebhard, Alson Clark, Wallace Neff. *Wallace Neff: Architect of California's Golden Age*. Santa Monica, CA: Hennessey & Ingalls, 2000.

Neff, Wallace. *Wallace Neff (1895–1982): The Romance of Regional Architecture*. Huntington Library, 1989. Reprint, Santa Monica, CA: Hennessey + Ingalls, 1998.

Newmark, Harris. *Sixty Years in Southern California*. 4th ed. Los Angeles: Zetlin & Ver Brugge, 1970.

Neuhaus, Eugene. *The Art of the Exposition*. Panama-Pacific International Exposition. San Francisco: Elder, 1915.

Newcomb, Rexford. *Franciscan Mission Architecture in Alta California*. New York: Architectural Book Publishing Company, 1916.

———. *Mediterranean Domestic Architecture for the United States*, (Acanthus Press Reprint Series). New York: Acanthus Press, 1999.

———. *Old Mission Churches and Historic Houses of California*. Philadelphia: J. B. Lippincott, 1925.

———. *Spanish-Colonial Architecture in the United States*. New York: J. J. Augustin, 1937.

———. *The Spanish House for America: Its Design, Furnishing, and Garden*. Philadelphia: J. B. Lippincott, 1927.

O'Melveny, Henry W. *Recollections of H. W. O'Melveny*. Los Angeles: Privately printed, 1989.

Ovnick, Merry. *Los Angeles: The End of the Rainbow*. Los Angeles: Balcony Press, 1994.

Peixotto, Ernest. *Romantic California*. New York: Scribner's, 1910.

Pitt, Dale and Leonard Pitt. *Los Angeles A to Z: An Encyclopedia of the City and Country*. Berkeley, CA: University of California, 1997.

Poe, Stanley. *Naples: The First Century (Naples, the City or Red Tile Roofs, the First Century, the Island)*. Stanley Poe, 2005.

Polyzoides, Stefanos, Roger Sherwood, and James Tice. *Courtyard Housing in Los Angeles: A Typological Analysis*. New York: Princeton Architectural Press, 1997.

Poole, Jean, and Tevvy Ball. *El Pueblo: The Historic Heart of Los Angeles*. Los Angeles: Getty Trust Publications, 2002.

Requa, Richard. *Architectural Details: Spain and the Mediterranean*. Cleveland, OH: J. H. Jansen, 1927.

———. *Old World Inspiration for American Architecture*. Denver, CO: Monolith Portland Midwest Company, 1929.

Rindge, Frederick H. *Happy Days in Southern California*. Cambridge, MA: Knickerbocker, 1898.

Robinson, W. W. *Los Angeles from the Days of the Pueblo*. Menlo Park, CA: Lane/California Historical Society, 1959.

———. *Ranchos Become Cities*. Pasadena, CA: San Pasqual Press, 1939.

Roderick, Kevin and J. Eric Lynxwiler. *Wilshire Boulevard: Grand Concourse of Los Angeles*. Santa Monica, CA: Angel City Press, 2005.

Rodriguez, Richard. *Brown: The Last Discovery of America*. New York: Penguin, 2003.

Smith, Bruce, and Alexander Vertikoff. *Greene & Green: Masterworks*. San Francisco: Chronicle Books, 1998.

Soule, Winsor. *Spanish Farm Houses and Minor Public Buildings*. New York: Architectural Book Publishing Company, 1924.

Starr, Kevin. *Inventing the Dream: California through the Progressive Era*. New York: Oxford, 1986.

———. *Endangered Dreams: The Great Depression in California*. New York: Oxford, 1996.

———. *Material Dreams: Southern California through the 1920s*. New York: Oxford, 1999.

Tuttle, Kathleen. *Sylvanus Marston: Pasadena's Quintessential Architect*. Santa Monica, CA: Hennessey + Ingalls, 2002.

Vogel, Steve. *The Pentagon: The Untold Story of the Wartime Race to Build the Pentagon and to Restore it Sixty Years Later*. New York: Random House, 2007.

Watters, Sam. *Los Angeles Houses, 1885–1919*. New York: Acanthus, 2007.

———. *Los Angeles Houses, 1920–1935*. New York: Acanthus, 2007.

Weaver, John D. *Los Angeles: El Pueblo Grande*. Pasadena, CA: Ward Ritchie Press, 1973.

Weitze, Karen. *California's Mission Revival*. Santa Monica, CA: Hennessey + Ingalls, 1984.

Wharton, Edith. *Italian Villas and Their Gardens*. New York: Century, 1904. Reprint, New York: Rizzoli (with The Mount Press), 2004.

Williams, Greg. *The Story of Hollywoodland*. Hollywood, CA: Papavasilopoulos Press, 1992.

Winter, Robert. *California Bungalow*. Santa Monica, CA: Hennessey + Ingalls, 1980.

———. *Toward a Simpler Way of Life: The Arts & Crafts Architects of California*. Berkeley, CA: University of California, 1997.

———. *Craftsman Style*. New York: Abrams, 2004.

Yoch, James. *Landscaping the American Dream: The Gardens and Film Sets of Florence Yoch*. New York: Abrams/Saga Press, 1989.

Young, Betty Lou. *Pacific Palisades: Paradise by the Sea*. Pacific Palisades, CA: Pacific Palisades Historical Society, 1983.

———. *Rustic Canyon and the Story of the Uplifters*. Pacific Palisades, CA: Casa Vieja Press, 1975.

———. *Santa Monica Canyon: A Walk through History*. Pacific Palisades, CA: Casa Vieja Press, 1997.

———. *Street Names of the Pacific Palisades and Other Tales*. Pacific Palisades, CA: Pacific Palisades Historical Society, 1990.

Zack, Michele. *Altadena: Between Wilderness and City*. Altadena, CA: Altadena Historical Society, 2004.

Acknowledgments

This book could not have been realized without the support of Charles Miers, David Morton, Douglas Curran, and Abigail Sturges. We are most grateful for their encouragement. We are also honored that Donald Waldie agreed to play so integral a role.

Our deep appreciation goes out to all of the homeowners who graciously shared their houses and stories, as well as to the following people for helping to make this book a reality:

Michael Berger
Brett Waterman
Thomas Blumenthal
Raun Thorp
Brian Tichenor
Virgil McDowell
Michael Burch
Diane Wilk
Joe Nye
Victoria Yust
Ian McIlvaine
Cindy Grant
Karen Hudson
MaryAnn Bonino
Lisa Blackburn
Bobbi Mapstone
Bruce Whiteman
Crosby Doe
Tim Gregory, *The Building Biographer*
Hennessey + Ingalls Art & Architecture Books
Arcana Books on the Arts
Frank Magallanes (digital technician)

Melba Levick
Douglas Woods
John McIntyre, Assistant Editor